U.S. Special Warfare

The Elite Combat Skills of
America's Modern
Armed Forces

Samuel A. Southworth

T0382437

DA CAPO PRESS

A Member of the Perseus Books Group

Published by Da Capo Press
A Member of the Perseus Books Group
http://www.dacapopress.com

Cataloging-in-Publication data for this book is available from the
Library of Congress.

ISBN 0-306-81357-2

Da Capo Press books are available at special discounts for bulk
purchases in the U.S. by corporations, institutions, and other
organizations. For more information, please contact the Special
Markets Department at the Perseus Books Group, 11 Cambridge
Center, Cambridge, MA 02142, or call (617) 252-5298.

First edition, first printing.

1 2 3 4 5 6 7 8 9—07 06 05 04

Printed and Bound in the United States of America.

Contents

Introduction   v

Chapter 1   Down These Dark Streets: Urban
Warfare   1

Chapter 2   Climb to Glory: Mountain Warfare   27

Chapter 3   Strike from the Sea: Amphibious
Warfare   52

Chapter 4   Whistling "Garry Owen": Cavalry   73

Chapter 5   Whispering Death: Snipers   95

Chapter 6   Spooks in G2: Military Intelligence   119

Chapter 7   Alone on the Battlefield: Escape
and Evasion   141

Chapter 8   Build and Blow: Combat Engineers   164

Chapter 9   Peacekeeping Paradox: Military
Operations Other Than War   186

Chapter 10   Secret Warfare: The Lure of Daring   207

Afterword   223

Bibliography   226

Index   228

Introduction

SERVING IN THE military in the early days of America was a pretty straightforward proposition. You had your musket, and kept it in good condition, and nearby, with one eye on the tree line as you ploughed up rocks from the poor soil of New England, or cleared a forest in Virginia, and once a week you went to the town common and drilled under a local squire who had been elected as commander of the local militia. Forming up in a straight line, dressing the ranks so it looked neat, and then marching took quite a bit of practice. The hope was that when faced with an enemy, your small group could provide a wall of bayonets and a steady rate of fire, even as you grappled with the complicated and slow loading process. In those early days, regular formations for pitched battle action were also accompanied by a series of irregular actions which most often involved moving across trackless forested hills trying to locate the enemy camp, and then engaging the enemy from behind the nearest tree or rock.

Whatever needed to be done to prosecute these small wars of colonial America could usually be accomplished by familiar faces from your town, be they blacksmiths, carpenters, ministers, boatmen, loudmouthed bar brawlers, genteel chaps who read *Plutarch's Lives*, or the local medical man. Because the musket was a necessity for hunting and self-protection, there were many men who could shoot darn well, and who knew the forest and how to slip through it without falling down holes or making a lot of noise.

There is a certain ad hoc charm to some of these early military outings by the colonials, leavened by the sometimes-tragic results. For instance, when Captain Lovewell led a band in 1725 from northern Massachusetts to Fryeburg, Maine, in search of revenge and scalps, they had God's own time just getting north of the big lake in New Hampshire and then following the Ossipee River over into Maine where they thought the local hostiles were holed up. And then instead of falling upon the native village like the wrath of God, they were surprised and attacked by a war party on the shores of what is now Lovewell's Pond near the Saco, and it was nip and tuck before they were able to disengage and straggle back to the south. This was hardly Frederick the Great on the warpath. They lacked the right clothing, good guides, any sort of intelligence, and soon found themselves well over their heads.

But by the time of the American Revolution, armies of the new United States began to exhibit a greater degree of professionalism, helped by teachers such as Baron von Stueben. The combination of special warfare skills such as ambushes and forced marches through wilderness areas, along with greater cohesion among troops and better commanders, made for a formidable force that was underestimated by the British and went on to secure the freedom of the new country.

Today this country has the most sophisticated army ever imagined on the face of the earth, and it is split into so many specialties and fields that you can be forgiven for thinking there isn't any way to get a handle on what they do these days. And yet there is a fairly simple method of comprehending everything you see on the nightly news or read in the newspapers, and, as historians are so fond of murmuring in the background, the path to understanding the future lies in fully understanding the past. While the new technology is always a bit off-putting, the nuts and bolts of how things get done on the battlefield are just the same as they ever were.

Courage cannot be replaced by a computer chip, and leadership in wartime has not changed one bit. What has changed are some of the terms and ways of thinking about military problems, and the nature of war itself is in a state of flux right now. But the roots of the American military system are evident in everything that it does, even if it is now a $450-billion-a-year operation that stretches from pole to pole. A colonial commander would think he had gotten into a bad barrel of rum if you tried to explain about nuclear submarines cruising the depths of the ocean, or satellites overhead sending back pictures and radio transmissions; but he wouldn't wonder at the utility of the systems—Captain Lovewell could have used a few satellite photos and some command and control guidance as he staggered along the Ossipee.

The task of the soldier hasn't changed all that much; as the USMC used to parse it, "See the hill, take the hill." And yet today we have separate branches for all the things that may need to be done in the field, and so many specialists that there are few privates left in modern armies—and they are even called "Specialists." This doesn't mean that there is any less danger in a war zone, but simply honors the fact that a great deal of additional training is needed for all the ins and outs of modern combat.

The purpose of this book is to explain just how complex modern military operations can be, while also always looking back to the past to explain why none of this is really "new." After all, we are not fighting giant bugs from outer space—yet. Contained within each of the chapters is a look back at the historical origins of these modern combat specialties. Each chapter tries to show, in non-technical language, just what the background is as well as examine how they operate in today's armed forces.

The title, "U.S. Special Warfare," is somewhat of a misnomer. Certainly when the U.S. Navy (in places like Little Creek and Coronado) speaks of special warfare they have a very specific concept in mind, and it doesn't include cavalry or peacekeeping. I take the term to mean warfare that is different enough in a crucial way to be removed from simply digging a hole, waiting for the right moment, and then surging forward. In modern combat, there is a much more complicated scenario being played out every time soldiers saddle up and go out the door. To understand just what they are doing, it helps if you have the history at your fingertips—from the Trojan horse to asymmetrical warfare. In warfare, there are any number of ways to skin a cat, and we shall look at how modern combat specialists do that— using their unique tricks of the trade.

We begin our tour with urban warfare, and then proceed along to fighting in mountains, going ashore from landing craft, the uses of mobility, be it horses or Bradley Fighting

Vehicles, pause for a long-range shot with the snipers, consider the difficulties of military intelligence, understand what it takes to survive behind the lines, blow a few bridges with the combat engineers, scratch our heads over the weird concept of peacekeeping, and then plunge into the black for covert and plausibly deniable ops in a secret war. At every step we will pause to consider the roots of each of these specialties, and see that while they are certainly tricky and dangerous, they are by no means new. Each chapter can be read by itself, although there is a progression that will be evident by the end, and none of it is meant as a manual for how to do any of these things, although some of the material comes from manuals.

As an author, my job is to read everything I can get my hands on, and then present it to readers in such a way that they will want to turn the page. With enough C4 almost anyone can blow up a bridge, but authors don't do that around their neighborhoods (or don't do it for very long), so some allowance has to be made for a civilian writing about these topics. I have made a good faith effort to understand each of these combat specialties as well as I could without actually doing any of them, and my goal has been to help you understand the specialized tasks of our soldiers better by exploring the historical and contemporary context of each topic. It is my hope that by understanding what we send these soldiers out to do, we will honor the tremendous sacrifice that they make (and have made) on our behalf.

"Qui desiderat pacem,
praeparet bellum."
— Vegetius

CHAPTER 1

Down These Dark Streets: Urban Warfare

IF YOU ASK professional military planners, leaders, and soldiers where they would least like to fight, the answer will almost always be: "In the streets." Despite the obvious problems with jungles, forests, deserts, mountains, and exposed plains, the notion of mixing it up in an urban setting doesn't appeal to anyone, and for very good reasons. The historical record is daunting, and the theoretical concerns are many. Cities (and towns) offer your enemy endless cover from which to pop up and pop you, lots of places to hide, as many chances for booby traps as there are urban features, and they restrict your mobility, communications, intelligence, and firepower. Add to that a civilian population that can be either openly hostile and/or placed in grave danger due to your operations, and you have a type of warfare that is at the top of the "must avoid" list.

One of the reasons the USMC excels at urban warfare is that they practice a great deal, such as here at the mock town in Quantico, VA. One guesses from this picture that some gruff sergeant is yelling about a threat from a rooftop. Notice how they are using the corner of the building to shield part of their bodies, although it is harder for the left-handed Marine in the center to deploy his weapon without exposing himself.

But our enemies know all this as well, and will often hunker down in a built-up area for all the advantages it offers to a defender. For this reason the U.S. military spends a great deal of time fighting their way through mock towns, honing their response to sudden hostile developments, and making sure that all parts of the offensive force are coordinated, from the rifle squad up to the regimental level. And like everything else, it has an acronym: MOUT (military operations urban terrain).

History provides us with a lengthy and frightening list of urban combats that have been incredibly hard on both sides, from the Crusaders at Antioch and Jerusalem to Napoleon's rough visit to Moscow, and right up through Stalingrad, Hue, Panama, Mogadishu, and Baghdad. With the development of fortified villages and then castles as the linchpins of city states, the same themes kept coming up. The defenders counted on making the attacking force restrict themselves to a killing zone (such as the narrow gate of a castle) where they would get bunched up and make a fine target for the defenders to kill from relative cover. On

Here we have Godfrey de Bouillon entering Jerusalem during the first Crusade. This imaginative print leaves to one side the terrible difficulties the Crusaders encountered in their crazed assault on the Holy Land, and the fact that many of them wouldn't be going home.

Urban warfare can make or break a reputation. Here we see the young Napoleon Bonaparte attacking a crucial fort in the anti-revolutionary town of Toulon, which was besieged from September 7 to December 19, 1793. During the climactic assault, Napoleon was wounded in the leg by a bayonet—but the fort was captured, which gave the French a secure place from which to shell the British fleet. Admiral Hood wisely sailed away, and Napoleon was promoted to general.

4

the other side, it seems as if it was pretty easy to get lulled into a siege mentality: "Well, they're all holed up in there, and all we have to do is make them surrender by either making their quality of life so abysmal that any reasonable person would hesitate to continue, or else force a breach in the walls or get a traitor to open a gate some dark night, and then pour in and slaughter them at will." Methods of making the defenders wish they were somewhere else included denying them food and water, and even using catapults to hurl disease-ravaged corpses over the walls at regular intervals. Oddly enough though, it often turned out to be the besieging force that ran out of quality of life, or found themselves attacked in the rear by a relief force that knew just where to find them.

With the vogue for fortifications that was spearheaded by the talented French engineer Vauban, the shape of a defensive position and the taking of that position came to be sort of a dance, a process where the defenders built in all sorts of clever touches such as walls that could cover other walls (hence the star shape of so many forts in the seventeenth and eighteenth centuries), moats and dry ditches to make the approach a hard slog, sharpened stakes to restrict attackers, and then boiling oil or water dumped on the heads of the attackers. But as far back as Alexander the Great (at the siege of Tyre) and then the Romans, there were already mighty siege machines that could be rolled forward to deploy a range of options, from ramps that allowed the attackers to flow onto the battlements, to battering rams for use on gates or walls, to work crews digging under the walls to make them collapse at just the right time. But if the way for an attacker to roll those machines forward was restricted, then they would have to begin digging a series of trenches, getting closer and closer to the hostile walls, just to ensure the safety of the attacking force so it could actually come to grips with the defenders.

And always at the sharp point of these restricted attacks there were the same themes: lack of room to maneuver, and a series of sharp combats that hinged on fate and destiny, and were often decided by lone individuals either holding a position despite all attacks (such as the brave Roman who held a bridge by himself because not enough of the enemy could get at him), or a particularly sharp assault led by a charismatic leader that would not be denied (such as Napoleon grabbing a banner and forcing the bridge at Arcola through his example and daring).

Urban warfare is connected to all of these because of the emphasis on choke points and restricted mobility. These two features make all the large and dramatic moves of classical and modern warfare come to a grinding halt. There were only a few commanders confident and savvy enough to bypass cities and strongholds and focus on conquering open land, trusting in their reserves to follow along and mop up defenders hiding in castles or towns. Part of this is also basic psychology, in that the capture (or fall) of a given city or stronghold can have an effect out of all proportion to the actual strategic importance of that spot on the map. Tsar Alexander knew this in 1812, when he and General Kutusov decided to first fight seventy-five miles to the west of Moscow, and then after the split decision at Borodino to abandon Moscow to the French army. Napoleon was evidently not only not feeling well, but he was also confounded to have captured this exotic legendary city and yet have no overtures of surrender be made to him or his staff by the other side. This episode is a fascinating glimpse into

Attacking earthworks head on is called "doing it the hard way." Here in the American Civil War, a Union company attacks uphill during the siege of Vicksburg in broad daylight. The flag is carried up front, picked up as each flag bearer was killed or wounded. The officer is leading from close to the front—and they are getting hammered.

how urban operations could bedevil one of the legendary commanders of history, and it's easy to see why. The French entered the city with very little resistance, and Napoleon installed himself in the central area as scattered small fights and fires broke out around him. There he sat in the Kremlin for weeks as the autumn slipped away, awaiting feelers of a truce, not able to see that the mere capture of this holiest of Russian cities was insufficient to accomplish his objectives

7

of forcing the Russians to adhere to his policy of not trading with the British empire. And while there has been a great deal of debate about who was actually responsible for the incineration of Moscow, it appears that the cranky and resolute mayor of the town did indeed wire the whole thing to go up in a fireball. At that point, Napoleon's grand trophy became a burning hell, and he himself had a fair amount of difficulty negotiating the narrow flaming streets to escape to the northwest, just prior to beginning one of the worst retreats on record.

Or consider the case of Verdun in World War I, which, while it didn't feature any urban combat, was entirely predicated in both the offense and defense on the absolute value of a rather drab eastern French city with precious little objective value. But as the German general Falkanhayn rightly predicted, and as French generals Joffre, de Castlenau, and Petain proved beyond all doubt, this was indeed the one place the Germans were willing to make one of their largest objectives, and the French were willing to cycle fully 80 percent of their entire forces through in order that it should not be taken. Costing a grand total of some 600,000 casualties (both sides included), Verdun stands today as a cautionary tale and a particularly savage example of the value (or lack thereof) of any given city. As the Germans knew and the French came to realize, the taking of Verdun would have been a dagger strike at the heart of France, and as such it became a killing ground that took on a life of its own.

World War II had quite a few cases of urban combat, and none of them more costly than the epic struggle for the industrial city of Stalingrad. Once again the Germans attacked a city that could have been bypassed (even though

The French artist Maurice Toussaint created this lovely poster in 1919, three years after the blood-soaked campaign of Verdun. It is meant to show not only the long-suffering French defenders, but also the battered but unbowed city itself, which the Germans had shelled extensively. But the bells still ring out from those steeples in the distance, and they did not pass.

9

it provided 25 percent of the tanks and vehicles of the Soviet army) in favor of the oil fields to the south, and yet it became a place that had to be taken (from the German point of view) and equally had to be defended no matter what (from the Soviet point of view). While German General Paulus fought his way with great difficulty to the city center between August and October of 1942, the wily Russian General Vasili Chuikov used every nuance and structure of the urban terrain to make the German artillery and air force less effective than it would have been in open terrain, giving up each building and intersection begrudgingly, and counting on his fanatic and dedicated Red Army to sacrifice themselves on a daily basis. Between the amazing bravery of the Soviets and the meddling of Hitler with his generals, this city fight became a staggering loss for the Germans and a turning point in the war. Just as at Moscow in 1812, Stalingrad was a city that wasn't worth taking, and provided the start of the end for another overly ambitious leader. The lessons are clear; not only are cities difficult and dangerous to fight in, but they can also swing the entire mood of a war dramatically by the outcome of the combat.

Despite their troubling features, cities have often loomed large in American military history, from the battles in the American Revolution to Basra and Baghdad. Leaders and planners and soldiers know that cities cause trouble, but because they are so often symbolic targets as well as real ones, they must be taken one way or another to achieve objectives of a larger strategic nature. George Washington knew he had to throw the British out of Boston, which he did with the help of the artillery from Ticonderoga, and he fought hard to keep the New York area, from Brooklyn to White Plains, but was unable to make a stand against the disciplined British forces at that stage of the war. He had signed off on the lunatic attack on Quebec by Benedict Arnold through the howling wilderness of Maine because that was how the British had tossed the French out of the New World twenty years before. And the Revolution ended with the siege at Yorktown, with the American troops able, with French naval and infantry assistance, to box up Cornwallis in an untenable position. But mostly the Americans tried to attack on open ground, except during surprise attacks like Trenton, knowing that fighting in built-up areas wouldn't be to their benefit.

Likewise, the Battle of New Orleans was fought south of that town where the British could be forced to approach a defended position over open ground; and some of the sharpest fighting (but not the decisive battle) of the Mexican-American War was in the cities of our southern neighbor—but once again, they had to be taken to force the enemy to believe themselves defeated. Sieges such as Vicksburg and Petersburg in the Civil War had all the familiar horrors of sieges, including massive artillery barrages on both sides, and costly assaults on strongly held positions. But it was the village and city fighting of World Wars I and II that made the Americans experienced and wary urban fighters.

By the time the War Department put out its handbook on German forces in March of 1945, the enemy's doctrine of city fighting was fairly well understood. The Germans would make sure their main defensive positions were well inside the city so they couldn't be inspected and shelled too easily, and then would try to organize a way to canalize an attacker into killing zones through obstacles and cul de sacs. Tanks might be used as static positions dug into a square or

Rushing ahead is a two-edged sword in urban combat. Here men of the U.S. 55th Armored Infantry Battalion and a tank from the U.S. 22nd Tank Battalion charge into a smokescreen set up by the burning building on the right. While their advance is covered by the smoke, you have to wonder who is waiting on the other side in this 1945 photo—probably some very experienced Germans. The tanker on the left is providing cover fire with an M2 .50-caliber turret-mounted machine gun.

crossroads, and in the meantime an irregular line of defense (to allow for flanking fire) would be set up in a maze of buildings and ruins, with passages hacked through the walls of adjoining buildings, and every window left open or broken, with the shooters placed in the center of the rooms to conceal their positions. Snipers would find locations with good concealment and field of fire, and everything that could be booby tapped would be booby trapped. The idea was to slow down and isolate attacking forces, the better to mop them up with mobile reserves. In all too many small

When the German commander of the town of Wesel dug in and forced a house-to-house fight, the result was a devastated moonscape as shown in this photo from April of 1945. The round pits are shell holes, indicating a barrage of some magnitude and duration, and indicate a cover bombardment for the attacking American troops, as a result of which most of the town was reduced to dust, except, curiously, the church in the right background.

villages and larger towns in Italy, France, and Belgium, the task of taking a German defensive position was one of dogged progress and guaranteed losses. They could be taken, but it wouldn't be easy. And as the Japanese had already shown a great talent for fanatic defense on any number of blood-soaked islands, it's pretty easy to see the

13

appeal of dropping a few atomic bombs on their civilians rather than settle in for an invasion of the homeland island and the promise of a great deal of urban warfare.

For reasons having to do with unfailing valor and an amazing record of combat success in the toughest arenas, the U.S. Marines have often been at the sharp end of the stick when it comes to fighting in cities, and they have done this from Peking (during the Boxer Rebellion) to Inchon to the cities of Vietnam and Panama and Iraq. In the worst-case scenarios, towns had to be cleared street by street, and building by building. But this is not to slight the U.S. Army, whose soldiers have also been called upon time and again to wade into an urban area and somehow pacify it. And, in the modern age, they have to watch out for the civilians who live there at every step of the way—they can't just flatten cities with firebombs—they'll have won the battle and lost the war of public opinion.

The current state of urban combat has some new wrinkles, mostly provided by technology, but the business of taking a town hasn't actually changed all that much. It begins with identifying towns and cities that are of strategic importance, and then gathering as much intelligence about them as possible. You'll want to know everything you can before you get there, including how the power grid is wired, if the sewers are large enough to operate in (consider the Special Forces troops who penetrated deep within Baghdad and came up through manholes), where the enemy is holed up, and where the civilians are concentrated. Then the decision can be made whether to bypass opposition, or if you need to tackle it head-on—but don't. The surest way to get killed is to simply march into a city.

Two Marines providing cover from a rooftop as their mates enter another building. They are also wearing gasmasks, which will make things easier for them when the village starts to burn, as they almost always do in warfare.

Instead of that, troops are needed who have been trained to operate in the strange urban environment, and that includes how to fight in streets, how to clear houses, how to isolate and neutralize pockets of resistance, and how defenders can be kept off balance by a mix of mobility and initiative. These troops will need to be constantly on the alert, and make

15

Here two U.S. Marines in Albania practice rushing forward while three fellow Marines cover them. They had better hope there aren't any hostiles in those windows to the left, or a machine gun stationed off to the right. This is in the courtyard of a building, and there are few more dangerous places for modern warriors than such a set up. They might have done better to blow through that wall on the left and clear the rooms from the inside, but sometimes speed carries the day.

their security and awareness of the cityscape their first priority.

Rifle squads are brought into action either by marching (least desirable) or by mechanized transport, such as Bradley Fighting Vehicles, M113s, Humvees, or helicopters. Helicopters have a great advantage, the same as the news chopper gliding above a freeway traffic jam, in that they can jump like knights in chess and deliver troops where the enemy will least expect them. They also place the troops where they most wish to be, that is to say on the top of buildings, because that is where you want to begin your clearing (not at ground level), and because of the lines of sight the tops of buildings offer. But as we have found out only too well, choppers are vulnerable and fragile beasts, and can quickly come a-cropper in urban terrain.

One recent military manual offers "Seven Life-Saving Rules of Movement," to wit: "1) Never allow yourself to be seen in silhouette, and keep low at all times; 2) Avoid open spaces; 3) Select your next position in cover before you make your move; 4) Hide your movements any way you can; 5) Move fast; 6) Stay clear of any covering fire; 7) Be alert and ready for anything." You can already see what a strain this places on troops. They need to use their ears as much as their eyes, and be ready to respond quickly to any signs of trouble, while staying concealed as much as possible. But with training, troops report that they get better at picking out good places to fire from, and that those places are from a prone position, or using the cover of rubble and debris, or from rooftops when they can get next to something like a wall or a chimney, or from the inside of a room, far enough inside to let them have a fair field of fire but to conceal the muzzle flash of their weapon as they fire it.

Doorways and windows are avoided if there is any reasonable way to do so—better to hack or blow a hole in a wall to gain entry, rather than to make themselves targets by coming in the expected way. In choosing where to fire their weapons from, they'll want to have the ability to make fast and accurate shots, and to do so from someplace that allows them to keep most of their bodies behind a protective feature. Note that protective features don't always stop bullets, but they can prevent the enemy from seeing the shooters as they send bullets their way.

For this reason camouflage is an important consideration, and in urban terrain there is both a day and night version. It may also be helpful to disguise the outline shape of one's helmet or rifle, by attaching branches or cloth with rubber bands. The precious few seconds gained may make all the difference in a firefight in a city. They need to watch out for basement windows, duck under any windows at their level, and when firing around corners, don't do it standing up-that's where the enemy would expect them to be. The rifle squad that can move quickly and safely into a town, identify the enemy's positions, and bring accurate fire to bear on those positions stands a good chance of living through urban combat. Physical fitness and training will be taxed to the limit.

Because any one soldier can carry only so much ammunition and grenades, a depot needs to move up as the rifle squads push into a city. It's very clear in military history that when things heat up, soldiers will become profligate users of ammo—and with good reason. A fair amount of firing in combat seems to be to reassure your team that you're still a viable entity, and to keep the other fellow's head down. As such, if it provides you with moral support and the ability to press on to the next good firing position, one is inclined to say "fire away." For crossing streets, alleys, and open spaces, the current doctrine seems to be to do it as a bunch, instead of the classic "covering fire and go one by one" method. The theory is that more targets spread out the enemy's efforts, and may make for less accurate shooting than one running man.

One of the worst ways to proceed down a street is the way the Americans did it in such cities as Aachen in 1944: two files on either side, each watching the other side. This is playing right into the defender's hands. You may as well send printed invitations. Instead of that, a combination of street teams and helicopter teams can, with proper intelligence and planning, move into cities and isolate the enemy into pockets where they can be cut off and mopped up. And each of these small units will need to have a person who is not only watching for snipers and strongpoints, but also coordinating with the troops to follow. This makes for a very complicated battlefield. Keeping track of where you are and working the radios and watching for hidden positions is sure to tire out the most enthusiastic individual soldier.

When clearing a building, you first have to be aware of booby traps, and hence avoid any obvious means of entry, such as doors and windows. Unfortunately, booby traps are as endlessly inventive as the enemy has time to make them, and cover a full range of dirty tricks and shrewd assessments of human nature. Some famous ones from the Eastern Front of World War II were the piano rigged to blow up when a key was played, and the drawer left open and wired to explosives, and the picture left askew on a wall, with a little wire running away from it. It's strange how,

Company D of the 1/325th Airborne Infantry Regiment is shown here using a hasty construction to practice their ability to spring from out of a doorway and cover the street in two directions. Their sergeant is just above the doorway ready to yell advice, and also indicate just one of the important parts of urban fighting—don't forget to look up.

even in a combat zone, most average humans will play a chord on the piano, or close the drawer, or straighten the picture. Modern wrinkles include a handgun, rifle, or helmet left seemingly unattended, which almost anyone would snatch up to either deny its use to the enemy or as a souvenir. Boom! Simple trip wires at the top of darkened stairs can provide a dangerous fall, or else pull a hand grenade out of an ordinary tin can, allowing its arming handle to fly off. The only way to avoid such pitfalls is to not move too fast, and watch for anything that is out of place, and any wire. But remember, speed is always of the essence in any combat engagement, so a line needs to be found between moving fast enough to keep the enemy off balance, but not so fast that you rush into prepared ambushes.

It is generally agreed that houses are best cleared from the top down. Almost all defenses will be geared to people coming up the stairs, so the best strategy is to land on the roof and blow or shoot a hole in the ceiling. If the defenders can be driven out into the street (and into the fire of the street teams), all the better. If helicopters aren't available, they may have to use ladders (if they can bring or find them), or an agile member of the team could climb a drainpipe. Grappling hooks with rope attached can also be used, but this is an incredibly tiring way of going up two or three stories. Fire escapes are enticing, but awfully exposed. However, once that first house is sorted out, they can proceed along the rooftops with part of their team, hopefully as tanks and fighting vehicles move up with their street teams.

As SWAT teams and counterterrorist units have found through the years, fighting within houses is a terrible business. To knock down a door and enter with any chance of

21

prevailing requires a minimum of three soldiers, a "kicker" and two "shooters" (actually three once the kicker gets done with his boot-based operation). In assaulting a door, the last thing to do is try the handle. Instead of that you should shoot the lock, or the hinges, and then go in like a house a-fire, shooting. Light switches are likely to be booby trapped as well—you'll want to pull the main fuse if there is still power to that part of the city, and rely on either night-vision goggles or try to get the other side to reveal themselves by forcing them to shoot. You need to keep flat against any walls, while also being aware that modern firearms can fire through walls without too much trouble, and as with corners out in the street, come around them slowly and low down where the enemy may not be looking for you. Can't you just throw a grenade ahead of you into every window and room you come across? Well, not if there are civilians or hostages present. Grenades are wonderful devices, but they have their limits, such as the fact that you can't carry a hundred of them, and that they will sometimes wound or kill people on your own side if used in restricted spaces. The only good thing about attacking a room is that it is unlikely that there will be more than ten people inside them who are hostile to you, due merely to space limitations.

There also needs to be a security detail left back up on the roof, which can cover the main entries if the enemy tries to bolt that way, and also to maintain radio and visual contact with the troops who are coming up, as well as the street teams. In the meantime, it is recommended that you mix up your pitches inside, and don't clear every room the same way. In some of them, shoot or kick the door, throw a grenade and rush in, the first person getting flat against a wall quickly to cover the room, and the second person searching visually very carefully. In the next room, try blowing a hole through the wall and going in that way. And all the time the team has to be talking to each other and making sure everyone knows where everyone else is located, lest you be surprised by your own people and shoot them by mistake. When a room is cleared, they need to shout that out, and mark it with chalk, tape, or paint. When it comes time to descend a floor, they are back to the restricted movements of a stairway, much like the gate of a castle, which is a prime place to booby trap and canalize an attacker. Perhaps rappelling down the stairwell will give an edge if there is a very brave member of the assault team—and then they must not forget to check the basement.

In modern campaigns, there has been an increase in communications between troops involved in urban combat, and some off-the-shelf radios have found themselves going from Radio Shack to a combat zone much more quickly than is usual for gear acquisition in the military. Current doctrine is to have every squad leader hooked up to a communications net, and in some cases each individual soldier. Although this makes for a lot of chatter if radio discipline isn't enforced, the sharing of information can make for a quicker and safer operation all the way around. In the future, UAVs (unmanned aerial vehicles) and such developments as software radios, ultra-wideband signaling, and array antennas might overcome some of the difficulties of broadcasting among buildings, and assaults these days are planned with avenues of communication in mind.

Our recent experience in Baghdad had some interesting features for those who follow MOUT, such as our fears that the city would be turned into an open-air death zone filled with civilians who looked just like the opposition. That has

U.S. Marines patrolling the streets of Haiti, as they have done for generations. Notice how exposed they are—and what are the intentions of that group on the balcony to the left? This sort of duty is hard on everybody, as it isn't a combat situation, but it is urban and has all the perils of urban warfare. The USMC fortunately excels at such difficult tasks.

indeed been the experience of American troops after the relatively easy first part of the war. But at the initial assault on Baghdad itself, we had great maps and satellite images, but almost no human intelligence (HUMINT) from inside the city beyond those few Special Forces chaps who came up out of the sewers. Thus we were reduced to what became known as "Thunder Runs" by battle tanks from the out-

24

skirts. Military planners consider such "trolling for enemy fire" to be among the least desirable ways to pinpoint hostile positions. As it turned out, the city was essentially undefended, so we were able to roll in without a building-to-building fight. But this is not to say that such combat will never come up again. The long and painful occupation has provided our troops with a great deal of experience in urban raids and house clearing, and as about 75 percent of the world's population is estimated to be living in cities by the year 2010, these sorts of urban combat issues are bound to come up again and again. The Russian experience in taking Grozny in 1994 is most instructive, in that their small-unit leadership was very poor, as was the training and marksmanship of the Russian troops, and the Chechan rebels were able to place themselves so close to the enemy that he couldn't safely use covering fire, and this ultimately forced the Russians to use massive and overwhelming fire-power to take the city, resulting in a public relations loss and the withdrawal of Russian troops from the area.

American soldiers tend to have excellent NCOs leading dedicated troops with fairly good shooting skills, and for those reasons we have done reasonably well in urban areas, Mogadishu excepted. And despite technology, the game of street fighting will always be the same: to move fast (but not too fast) in a coordinated way that probes and isolates hostile positions, while clearing buildings and houses and eventually streets and neighborhoods until a city can be said to have been taken. It will never be anything other than difficult and dangerous.

That's the basic idea, and you can see why a great deal of training and good old-fashioned physical fitness is needed to make troops into city-clearing professionals. The U.S.

military spends a lot of time on these tasks, because of the great likelihood that we will have to fight in other cities in the future. There are about a dozen mock towns scattered throughout the states, and many more "Killing Houses" where these skills can be practiced under the watchful and judgmental eye of sergeants who know that sweat in training will save blood in combat.

CHAPTER 2

Climb to Glory: Mountain Warfare

THERE ARE FEW givens in warfare, but several of them deal with hills and mountains. First, a wise British officer said that it was most likely that your area of interest would be a hill where two maps met, if not in the corner of four adjoining maps. Second, it almost always seems that every attack is uphill. It used to be said that U.S. Marines were limited in their higher tactical thinking to the simple phrase: "See the hill; take the hill." Be that as it may, in today's conflicts there are always terrain considerations, and these can range from little hummocks to the massive mountains of the Hindu Kush, whose towering peaks are almost as high as Mount McKinley in Alaska. Mountain warfare is one of those classic concerns whose lessons are ignored at our peril, and whose history runs along remarkably consistent lines.

27

Commanders who understand and work well with mountains are among the legends of military history, and those who fail to remember the harsh lessons wafted down from blood-soaked slopes will also fail completely as they leave the flatlands and press on to the heights.

From our earliest records mankind has linked mountains with warfare, using them as defensive barriers and strongholds, or else passing over and through them in varying degrees of audacity in order to appear where they are least expected. The ancient hill forts throughout the British Isles are good examples, as are the fortified prominences scattered across the Middle East. The British model was a lozenge-shaped fort with a ditch dug around it and a palisade of sharpened logs, and then an internal keep at the high point for a last refuge should the outer walls be breached. Oddly enough, Green Beret camps on hilltops in Vietnam showed many of these same features, although the helicopter and machine gun had changed the tempo and progress of modern battle.

In many of the famous battles of the ancient Greeks the role played by heights of land is driven home again and again, be it the narrow beach of Marathon, or the cunning secret pass that the Persians used to fall on the rear of their enemy at Thermopylae. Interestingly, that pass was shown to them by a traitorous local, a theme we shall be getting back to in due time. Hills could even play a part in naval battles, as when the Greeks hid part of their fleet behind a hilly island at the battle of Salamis and then surged out to take the Persian fleet in the flank. Indeed, the Acropolis itself is a hilltop fortress with a narrow and easily defended entryway, and anyone who has studied the steep sides can see that it

Mountain warfare offers many advantages to attacking troops, as well as perils. Here the army of Alexander the Great uses a gnarly rock cliff to attack Porus's citadel in 325 BC, with the hope that Porus can't imagine anyone clambering up and over this tricky route. The U.S. 10th Mountain Division did much the same thing at Riva Ridge in Italy during World War II—and they did it at night.

29

was custom made for defensive purposes. It may be that the children's game "King of the Hill" has its roots far deeper in our collective psyches than has been considered.

Alexander the Great and Julius Caesar were among the legendary commanders who well understood how to work with the terrain they found, be it the hills of Gaul and Germany, or the mountains all the way to India. Given the choice, both would take the high ground and use the view from there to better understand the flow of their own attack or the attempts by an enemy to close with their forces.

Hannibal's famous end run on the Romans is perhaps the most famous of the ancient mountain campaigns, and while some details of his route are disputed, it seems that he cunningly followed the Rhone River up and then hanged a right into the Alps, picking up local guides as he went—of greater and lesser degrees of reliability. Some of the local people attacked him as he passed through their lands, often by setting traps in narrow defiles where spears, arrows, and rocks could be hurled down on the encroaching force to punch their passports in a definitive way.

Here it will be useful to pause for a moment and consider how mountains are formed and how they are used by military forces, because there isn't just a generic "mountain" that is always the same, despite some themes of weather and route finding that are tried and true. Mountains are either thrust up by tectonic plate action (where land masses collide and one of them is forced up while the other is forced down), or else they are worn down from the action of previous upthrust and the passage of water which can wear massive canyons through them over millions of years. There are a few monadnocks (named for Mount Monadnock in New Hampshire), which are peaks

Here we see Kabul, Afghanistan, in 1840. Seems like a nice town, doesn't it? But look at those mountains; this hostile landscape has provided a grave for many brave soldiers, from the Macedonians of 300 BC to the British in the 1800s to the Americans of the 21st century, as well as the scene for many desperate fights.

that exist seemingly on their own, but mostly mountains come in clumps and bunches, connected by ridges and separated by valleys and gorges. Today small and intrepid teams can pass over and through ranges of mountains, but that passage is often not an option for an army, where slow-moving pack trains and soldiers untrained in mountain movement will experience great difficulty in forcing their way over high peaks and ridgelines.

Rocks can vary from massive steep faces to an enormous pile of small stones (called "scree"), and neither is very welcoming to movement of large forces. Sometimes there is a ridge that can be followed to where you want to go, but often ridges connect high peaks and will expose troops to unpredictable winds and bad weather, so it would seem that the safest way to move through mountains is to follow the biggest rivers. A good way to understand this is to look at the highway and rail systems in the United States and Canada, and realize that the brilliant engineers who laid them out had a daunting task in finding routes that didn't become too steep for vehicles to negotiate. I-70 through the Colorado Rockies and I-80 through the Sierra Nevada in California are good examples, with only a few places where they had to resort to tunnels, but even then these roads are often shut down in winter to everything that doesn't have chains.

Note how many roads and highways follow rivers as far as they can, and often with wonderfully scenic results. And keep in mind that those engineers (many with military training) tramped and staggered through those mountains for months searching for passes and ways to force a route through. But remember that military operations can happen with a very short warning period, so if you don't have good maps or local guides, your passage through mountains can be a long and meandering one, with many false starts and blind canyons that do not lead where you think they will. Also, if you stick with the river, you will open yourself up to attacks from your high flanks, as Hannibal discovered in the Alps, much the same as the Russians in Afghanistan during the 1980s, and U.S. troops in the current war. So, the usual drill is to move people and equipment through the valleys, while scout and recon units pass along the flanking heights to ensure security. This was the model the Russians finally adopted in their bloody war for control of the Hindu Kush, and even then they came to grief fighting the tribes who had occupied those bitter mountains for thousands of years and beaten every force that dared venture into their land.

When William the Conqueror splashed ashore in October of 1066 and encountered King Harold at Hastings, he saw that the British infantry were gathered on a hill. Harold lost that battle because he was unable to control his ad hoc army, such that one wing was drawn off the hill by a localized success against the Normans, and were quickly cut down by the mounted French knights. A false retreat is a very old tactic that has proven to be evergreen, and was used by Napoleon at Austerlitz in 1805, as well as by the Sioux and Comanches in the American west. If you can sucker an enemy off his high ground, and then take it yourself, often you can turn the tide of battle.

During the American Revolution the various hills and mountains of the eastern colonies provided a veritable seminar in the use of terrain, from Dorchester Heights to the hills of Brooklyn to the ravine at 120th Street on the west side of Manhattan to the hills around Bennington and Saratoga to King's Mountain in South Carolina. The extraordinary line of hills that bisect the Hudson River at West Point made it the Gibraltar of the New World, with Storm King on one side and Breakneck Ridge on the other. As a result of the narrowing of this great river and the proximity of the mountains on either side, not only could a chain be stretched across to inhibit the passage of ships, but cannon could be brought to bear on any vessel so unwise as to try to force that narrow and twisting passage. One has only to stand by the river at West Point or look west from Breakneck Ridge to appreciate how this chokepoint worked. And the Americans, from their use and passage of the land for the shipping of goods to remote locations, often showed an astonishing ability to work with the landscape, be it Colonel Knox bringing the artillery from Ticonderoga to Boston, or Benedict Arnold forcing his way over the height of land that marks where the Dead River leads upstream to

Canada in his doomed attack on Quebec. He might have done better had he studied General Wolfe's attack of twenty years previous, when a small footpath had enabled the British to appear on the Plains of Abraham where the enemy hadn't expected them to be. If you can climb quickly enough, mountains can allow you to do seeming magic tricks that will cause your enemy no end of surprise.

Napoleon is a classic case of a general whose massive gifts for warfare included not only the ability to muster men and cannon where he was least expected, but also an inherent ability to understand landscape and how to use it for his own ends. In battle after battle it was so often the case that he had seen and understood the terrain better than his adversary, and during the years of his greatest victories there was hardly any opposing commander who could move across the landscape as sure-footedly as he could.

American history frequently features mountains, and often with the use of guns. It was the fur-trapping mountain men in their solitary meandering who discovered South Pass in Wyoming, where the wagon trains were to force a road through the Rockies, and the hill folks of Appalachia often proved to have an unerring feel for both landscape and shooting, as proven by Sergeant Alvin York in World War I. In the Civil War the importance of hills and valleys came up time and again, and generals like jaunty cavalrymen J. E. B. Stuart and Stonewall Jackson in the Shenandoah proved to be able to slip through the hills like will-o-the-wisps, using not only better maps but also a feeling for where the enemy would or could be, and where he himself was least expected. By using infantry who could march almost as far as cavalry, Jackson time and again befuddled his opponents, and was able to do things like feign a with-

The price of glory, as shown by Confederate dead at Little Round Top, one of the fiercely contested topographic features of Gettysburg. This "wet collodian" photo on glass is part of a stereographic pair, which when viewed with a special device jumps into 3D, making it even more horrifying. This was the "high-water mark" of July 2, 1863.

drawal while leaving artillery in a shallow valley to strike the bluecoats in the flank as they pursued the main body. In this campaign Jackson was able to tie up an inordinate amount of the enemy because he knew those hills and could pass through, around, and among them with a familiarity that flummoxed his less-gifted foes.

And of course throughout the battle of Gettysburg there is a constant theme of who owned what hills, and which flanks could be turned. The 20th Maine's daring action on the second day secured the Union's left flank amidst a tangled series of hills and declivities, while Pickett's ill-fated charge across the valley and uphill on the third day marked not only the high-water mark of the Confederacy, but also Lee's astonishing loss of cleverness in making what was ultimately a futile and fruitless gesture.

It could be argued that much of Teddy Roosevelt's public acclaim was won at San Juan Hill, although the attack was actually one hill over. But that minor action was easily understood by the Hearst-reading masses: an American commander had assaulted fortified blockhouses on a hilltop and prevailed. By the time Teddy was thrust into public prominence by assassination, people already had a feel for what made TR tick, and that included being able to execute one of the hardest of all maneuvers: the hill assault.

World War I was a watershed in so many ways, mostly in deadly killing technology advancement and horrific slaughter leading to and growing from stagnating trench warfare, but in another way it was hardly any different than the history of warfare up till then and since. The troops who held the high ground had a vastly better time of it, and it is to the German's strategic credit that all along the lines they almost always placed themselves where they could shoot down on the British, French, Belgian, and later American troops. There is a landscape panorama by a French artist of the Western Front that shows the entire line from the English Channel to Switzerland, and all along the way you can see the Germans dug in where the hills begin. And from even a casual reading of Erwin Rommel's great book *Infantry Attacks*, the training and emphasis on high ground that the Germans inculcated among their officers comes through time and again, from his trench raids in France to the actions he fought on hills and mountains in Romania. But tactical brilliance alone is never enough. In all too many cases, a successful assault on a mountain is followed by the German troops freezing on the heights in thin uniforms and bad weather. Be that as it may, Rommel shows the grasp of terrain and the inherent feel for how to move through it that has always marked the great commanders.

In Italy the Austrian invasion was followed by a lengthy series of back and forth battles, such as the Isonzo, and it is here that much of modern mountain warfare got its first concentrated development. The use of light artillery and mortars on mountains reached new levels of perfection, and such tried-and-true methods as the shelling of overhanging snow and ice to cause an avalanche on the enemy first became possible—a tactic still in use in the disputed Kashmir mountains between India and Pakistan.

At about the same time, civilian mountaineering had gained greatly in popularity, so that not only were there special troops such as the French Chasseur Alpine, the Italian Sardinian Brigade, and the German Wurtemburg Regiment, but the ways of the hills were starting to be of interest to gentleman adventurers as well as people who lived outside of mountainous areas. This resulted in better equipment as well as a deeper understanding of the ways in which mountains could be used to pursue military ends. Ancient peoples, from the Greeks to Native Americans, did not climb mountains for sport. It was thought that the gods lived on the heights, and would deal harshly with anyone who showed up lacking the right attitude. The climbing of the Matterhorn in Switzerland in 1865 was a galvanizing event due to the book *Scrambles Amongst the Alps* by the British explorer Edward Whymper. But it should be noted

Men of the U.S. 370th Infantry Regiment are shown here passing through the town of Prato, Italy, during April of 1945. Most roads in mountainous areas run along the valley, as shown, but if this had been more heavily defended they would have had to get up on those ridges to the left and right and move along them to prevent ambush.

that the ascent of that sharp-edged peak was accompanied by the loss of more than half the climbing party on the descent due to a stumble and a broken rope. By the 1930s many of the most famous mountains in the Alps had been climbed, and not a few by military men on furlough, such as the humorless and unlucky Germans who forced their way up the North Face of the Eiger, with not a few casualties along the way. Also, expeditions had been launched into the Himalayas, paving the way for the eventual summit success on Everest in 1952. Interestingly, Eric Shipton, who had done much of the mapping and scouting of the route used in 1952 was bypassed for leadership of the team, which was given to a military man, Sir John Hunt, in the belief that he would do a better job on the logistics and planning of such an assault. And in a curious reflection on the rise of Special Forces, today we have small groups moving quickly on mountains instead of the long logistic tail that accompanied Sir Edmund Hillary on his climb of Everest.

At each step of the way, as civilians and military men on holiday made the mountains more and more of a sport to be studied closely, the lessons learned and the gear proven to be useful was passed by osmosis to mountain troops. Everything from boots to pitons to crampons to rope was tried and adopted by the military, with the result that when World War II rolled around there were some of the best-equipped and most-experienced men serving in mountain units, and the lessons of the peaks had been taken to heart by the commanders.

In the United States, the 10th Mountain Division was the first specialized unit to have the patch on their shoulders that simply says: "MOUNTAIN." This was the result of a few visionary civilians rightly thinking that troops who were trained in climbing and skiing and snowshoeing could be as helpful to the American war effort as the Finnish ski troops had been in their fights with the Russians, during which they decimated the Soviet army by ghosting through the winter wonderland on skis, dressed in white, using the cold and dark and hills as their allies.

In the worst-case scenario, all troops who are needed and present are mountain troops—and just as with Rommel's command, often they freeze and get lost and generally consider the mountains to be a kind of frozen hell. But WWII mountain troops were often of exceedingly high caliber, such as the British Army and Royal Marine Commandos who trained on the rainy hills of Scotland and accomplished astonishing feats of bravery, and the German mountain

troops who learned to ski at Aarlberg and wore the eidel-weis flower on their caps proudly. They had the training, the boots, the clothing and gear, and the leadership to force their way up almost any peak and quickly transform a hostile environment into one that they could use for their own purposes, and to the enemy's dismay.

The Americans chose Colorado as their training ground, and it was there that the skiers, lumberjacks, climbers, and

The 10th Mountain Division stands ever ready to serve on the heights anywhere in the world—here, a member is seen training in Djibouti. This is one hard way to cross a ravine on a rope. If you had the time and gear, it would make it easier if you rigged up two lines and made a harness to sit in as you pull yourself across. Note this sergeant is on belay, the dark line going from his waist to a safety line above him out of shot.

ordinary folks like Bob Dole from Kansas came to learn and relearn the lessons of the hills. At places like Riva Ridge in Italy, the 10th Mountain Division proved it was the equal of any mountain warfare unit in the world, and just as with Wolfe at Quebec, it was proven again that using the cover of darkness and an unusual path to a height could put the enemy at a grave disadvantage. All it took was a great deal of training and gumption, as well as tough men and superior leadership.

The U.S. Army on Guadalcanal and the Marines on Okinawa and Iwo Jima had to learn hill assault the hard way, by trial and error. But it was in Korea that most American troops got the chance to really experience hill fighting in a protracted conflict. The Korean peninsula is almost all hills in the middle and north, and as a result nearly every day featured a lesson in the use of terrain, as well as the limitations of hill fighting. The folds in the earth between ridges can hide an enemy from your artillery, and the bad weather can shut down even the most ardent assault. Ridgelines and spurs became the everyday currency of that war, and holding and taking hills was how the troops came to know the land. Very few American troops had any sort of specialized mountain training, but they

Frostbite casualties from the "Frozen Chosin" of the Korean War, some of the men of the 1st Marine Division and the U.S. Army Seventh Infantry Division, who staged an epic retreat in December of 1950 in the dead of winter and against staggering odds. Notice the typical Korean landscape behind them.

quickly adapted to the land, and saw that it was just as true as ever—attacking uphill is very hard.

In Vietnam, the landscape was once again a major player, from the lowland jungles to the misty mountains on the borders with Laos and Cambodia. In that war for the first time there was the widespread use of helicopters, and this meant that Green Beret A Teams could be dropped onto a hilltop and resupplied by air, in a new wrinkle on the British hill forts of the Dark Ages. And Special Forces such as SOG and the Long Range Reconnaissance Patrols (Lurps) learned how to move among the overgrown hills and valleys anew, just as Roger's Rangers had two hundred years before.

Patrols would often be dropped on a ridge after a series of false landings to confuse the watching enemy, and then for up to a week search for the troop concentrations, always moving, trying to match the maps up with the terrain, and trying to avoid too much contact. Once again an old lesson came to the fore: moving on the ridges was the quickest way to go, but the water for survival was down in the valleys. Following a straight line meant an exhausting day of clambering up, over, and down the hills, whereas a path that followed the landscape could cover a greater distance and ensure some degree of safety. Also, helicopters often had a hard time due to the weather and the mountains, a condition acknowledged by pilots using the laconic phrase "There's rocks in those clouds."

Modern-day mountain warfare is an ancient art with a foot in the past and a foot in the future. As we have seen in the recent military actions in Afghanistan, and because so much of the world is not flat and level, America will always have need of special troops and training to enable us to climb and fight wherever an enemy might hide. Today this training goes on all over the country, from western Georgia (where the U.S. Army Rangers run their cliff assaults) to the Sierra Nevada (where the U.S. Marines train at Pickle Meadow) to Alaska (where Fort Greely provides not only mountains but an extra degree of cold and wet) to Fort Drum in New York state (where the 10th Mountain Division is based) to the Ethan Allen Firing Range in Vermont, where even ROTC members can get their first taste of fighting on slopes. Hannibal and Napoleon would have understood and approved of the modern curriculum. It starts with understanding the mountains as they are, in all their beauty

43

and harsh reality. A sloping wet surface never gets any more stable to cross, so they learn how to do it in all conditions while wearing a heavy pack and carrying a rifle.

Mountain ranges often create their own weather systems, with the high peaks acting as magnets for clouds and wind. Conditions can go from sunny and hot to freezing sleet in less than an hour—and then there's the wind. Wind is a killer because it sucks warmth out of a body even more quickly than cold, and when you add wet, you have a real problem with hypothermia, which is the loss of body heat that can quickly kill the most robust person. How much wind is too much? Among mountaineers it is a given that winds much above 45 mph will make walking difficult. Living as we do in houses and apartments, most of us don't have much experience with what a truly bad wind is like. How high can it go? The highest recorded wind is 242 mph, which was clocked on Mount Washington in New Hampshire in the 1930s—and that was just before the measuring apparatus blew away.

Fortunately, the world of civilian mountaineering and its lessons have been internalized by modern mountain troops, in that many of the instructors and commanders have done quite a bit of extreme hiking in their spare time, including expeditions to the Himalayas and Patagonia. As a result, the Marines have some of the finest mountain boots ever made,

One thing about mountain warfare—if it isn't downhill, the target will definitely be uphill! Here a U.S. Marine follows the tracks of his squad as he uses snowshoes to ascend a slope. But perhaps he should take the time to put white paint on his gear and weapon, and be using that treeline in the background as a sneakier way up? You feel mighty exposed in one of those big snowy fields.

and such wonder products as Gore Tex, fleece, and polypro are now standard issue. These are important because they form the heart of the layering system, which has proven to be the best way to beat wind and cold and damp. It starts with a layer next to your skin that is thin and light, and wicks moisture away from the skin as you sweat. Next is the fleece, including wind-blocking fabrics, which insulate and pass the wet to the next layer, which is windproof Gore Tex that not only blocks the wind but also allows the damp to pass to the outside and evaporate away. A large portion of the body's heat is lost through the head and extremities, so good hats and gloves and socks are part of the gear. And all of this is before anyone starts throwing ammunition, food, water, and medical supplies into their pack.

Troops are introduced to steep terrain slowly, starting with hill walking. How hard could that be? Well, you can slip on almost anything, so how you place your boots as you travel is actually of the greatest importance, and how you choose your route will often dictate how you must place your boots. A steep slope is best approached in a zigzag motion, now left, now right, rather than straight up, keeping your weight over your boots for balance, not leaning into the hill. In snow and ice, you may have to kick steps or cut them with an ice axe, which is also used for self-arrest

A U.S. Marine using his ski poles to steady his M-16A2 rifle with an M-203 40mm grenade launcher. Notice the use of blotchy white to make his weapon blend in. He is wearing a balaclava (a one piece polypro head warmer) and insulated gloves. He'll also have to remember to drink plenty of water while he's moving around the mountains in winter—dehydration is even more of a threat here than it is during a hot summer's day.

47

Men of the 10th Mountain Division get out of their trucks to clear a hilltop in the village of Orgun-E in Afghanistan. They are setting up a perimeter just prior to moving out. In some cases they were attacked at just such a place—arguing for a different style of infiltration, such as on foot, at night, and off a road.

after a slip. Failure to do so on a sufficiently steep slope will mean a long slide and injury or death.

Acclimatization is needed because anywhere much over five thousand feet the average human will get a headache and feel listless because of the lessening of oxygen in the air. The only way to overcome this is to spend time at higher altitudes before actually trying to do anything, a lesson that would seem to argue against having the 10th Mountain Division based at Fort Drum which is at 2,500 feet. The British make a point to go to Norway for some of their mountain training, and some of the difficulties reported from Afghanistan would seem to be directly related to acclimatization issues. The only thing to do is to make sure that troops get plenty of time to work at higher altitudes before throwing them into a serious mountain campaign.

Every facet of military activity is made more difficult by the addition of high icy mountains, so that simple things like shelter and water are of vital importance. Modern mountaineering tents are cleverly made to be dug into snow as a further barrier from the wind, and have vestibules for drying wet clothing. Mountain stoves need to be well made because it takes longer to boil water at great heights, meaning that they must be reliable and you have to carry a great deal of fuel. Eating snow isn't an option—it just makes you colder.

Sunglasses are not a fashion statement on mountains. People have gone snowblind in a remarkably short time from the glare off the white surface, and at higher altitudes the sun's rays are even stronger than at the beach. Troops are taught to make goggles if they must, including the Eskimo version which are mere slits cut in tree bark. It can be seen from this small point that mountaineering, and especially military mountaineering, is a game of details. Lose your gloves and you're out of luck. Take the wrong spur and you'll have to retrace your path when it deadends at a cliff. Try to cross a snowmelt-swollen mountain stream without ropes and you'll start losing personnel quickly. Medical evacuations will be very hard, and you may not have the air support you'd like due to weather and terrain.

Keep in mind the extreme youth of most of our troops—middle-aged guys would never be able to do all this stuff. Here a young 10th Mountain private covers his front while awaiting orders to move forward into Shuranam, a little village in Afghanistan. He is heavily armed, well-trained and led, and willing to obey orders and do what is needed to track down terrorists.

50

Bullets are affected by being fired up or downhill, and artillery may not be able to get up to where the fighting is taking place.

Military groups in the mountains have to rely on excellent training and superb leadership, often in small groups, to accomplish their missions. You can always tell who has had the training and who hasn't: the well-trained mountaineers are warm and well-fed and hydrated, are keeping an eye on the weather, don't willingly pass under avalanche slopes, don't travel on the ridgeline but below it where they will not be silhouetted against the sky by an enemy watcher, and can move with great speed and deftness over scree, wet boulders, icy slopes, and even sheer cliffs. And when they get to where the enemy is, they can move around and between them, and force them off prime real estate.

In the fighting in Afghanistan all the old lessons came back, including the difficulty of fighting mountain people on their home turf, where they had previously whipped both the British and the Russians. There has also been anecdotal evidence that some of our troops were attacked as they got out of their trucks, which doesn't seem to validate that commander's sense of securing the area. But the men of the 10th Mountain Division, as well as the Royal Marine Commandos, Canadian Special Forces, and U.S. Marines from Pickle Meadow, proved once again that even given a few false starts, modern mountain troops are the equal of any force that has fought for the high ground throughout history.

CHAPTER 3

Strike from the Sea: Amphibious Warfare

IN THE STAID civilian world, why does everybody want to live on the water? From the Texas border with Mexico hooking around Florida and right up to Lubec, Maine, and from Tijuana to British Columbia, it seems as if every blank spot is slowly being filled in, either by mansions, or high-rise condos with views of the restless waves. And this despite the fact that insurance companies in their ultimate wisdom are more and more reluctant to endorse policies that rely on the ocean behaving in any responsible way.

In the military realm, there has never been any debate about the use and utility of controling the seas, defending the coast, or landing on hostile beaches, as well as the ability to put ashore little teams for raiding or reconnaissance. With its past inextricably linked to the waves, and perhaps a good chunk of the future bundled into some sort of amphibious capability, it should come as no surprise that the United States has spent a great deal of time and treasure working on how to defend beaches, as well as how best to penetrate them with everything from a lone swimmer to division-plus scale assaults.

Amphibious operations combine most of the dangerous things in the world into one problematic package: wind, weather, water, and waves, always dicey to contend with, and then the unwelcome patter of hostile fire making your outing to the beach more than annoying. It can't quite be proven that more soldiers (and sailors and marines) have been killed just getting to the high-water mark as were ever slain on the beaches, but it would be a natural conclusion if you were to troll through military history and carefully look at just what it means to strike from the sea.

There may also be some facets of this type of warfare that encourage overly optimistic thinking, such as the big swaths of blue just out to sea, which look more inviting and amenable of maneuver than attacking the enemy through a swamp, and the fact that beaches seem like great places to rally a large group of men and get all their gear together for the push inland. But in hardly any other type of battle are there as many dangerous and unexpected influences at work as there are when the decision is made to hit the beaches.

Just ask the Persians at Marathon in 490 BC. They got ashore all right in Marathon Bay, managing to put about 25,000 men on dry ground without opposition. The Athenians had been sucked away from their city to deal with this landing force, and found themselves outnum-

53

A Victorian view of the battle of Marathon, in 490 BC. These sort of stylized views tell us more about the 1800s than about the Greeks—for instance, the shields and helmets are of the wrong type, being Roman of 500 years after Marathon. But the danger of arrows shot high in the air is accurate, and some of the fierce ardor of the Greeks comes through, as they were busy throwing the Persians off this beach.

bered almost two to one, as well as having no cavalry or fleet of their own to bring to the table. The Persians then sent all their horses and part of their fleet on a long end run to Athens, counting on bashing the Greeks right there before going on to make their city a franchise of Persia. But even outnumbered, the Greek flanks managed to win their local headbutting, and then turned on the Persian center, causing a massive retreat. And then there was trouble on the sand, as the Asiatic invaders were forced at spear and sword point back into the sea. Some drowned or were killed in nearby swamps, and seven of their ships fell to the Athenian war machine.

In the aftermath, the Greeks managed to hightail it back to town, and the Persians limped home to tend their resentment of these early democrats who fought like wolves when their homeland was threatened. When you don't have a good way to retreat, the failure of a large military mission against a shore can be more damaging than almost any other outcome short of wholesale slaughter.

Throughout history most of the ocean-borne attacks that worked were unopposed landings, such as Caesar and William the Conqueror slogging ashore on the British Isles. And the exposed position of island nations has been a theme down through the years. If the ocean surrounds you, then danger is there at every place where the waves touch your land. And think of the difficulty in predicting just where a hostile force will come ashore. For this, consider General Wolfe's assault on Quebec, where a landing party of highlanders used a little-known goat track to get up on the Plains of Abraham and behind the fortifications that Montcalm had used so well to protect his linchpin city from attackers on the St. Lawrence. The amphibious option enabled Wolfe to appear where he was not expected, and to triumph even at the cost of his life. Often the target of an aquatic attack will be a strategic point that will change the outcome of world history, which is one of the only reasons to even consider such a reckless maneuver.

And hardly any military landing force goes ashore on a nice day with a flat sea and gentle breezes blowing; all too often there are massive waves, a howling gale, shifting currents, and hidden sandbars. Attacks have gone to the line of departure and headed onto the beach on days when even hardcore surfers with wetsuits would be hiding in their vans. There is a telling picture of British forces taking their longboats ashore in east Africa in the 1830s, and the size of the waves is staggering. In these conditions ordinary boats (which in the olden days were mostly pointed at both ends) would be subject to all manner of cocked up outcomes, from having their sterns pushed sideways in such a manner that

55

a rollover was the very next thing that would happen, to "pitch poling," which is when a wave picks up a boat and slams the bow far down into the water, in the worst-case scenario striking and lodging on the bottom, and ejecting all the passengers at high speed and on a considerable trajectory. Modern-day SEALs and others who make a living going into bad places have the same options that the old-timers had: you can try to surf the waves in, and then row back into the next incoming wave to prevent it from smashing you to salty smithereens, or you can use a drogue anchor, which is an anchor that streams out aft and keeps your nose straight by pulling against the water, or you can wait and try to find the lull that almost always comes between sets of waves, as swimmers have long known, and then row like blazes to try to get to dry land before the next set comes crashing in.

Americans have always been at home on the water, and that includes many disparate bodies from Paul Revere crossing the Mystic River in 1775 to the divisions that waded ashore in the harbor at Inchon in 1950. As he was figuring out what an army would need in the Revolution, General Washington wisely tapped the experienced boatmen from Marblehead, Massachusetts, when he needed to go places not on a white horse, but by being rowed. This helped him out no end such as when he had to leave the borough of Brooklyn in 1776 and make his way to Manhattan, coming ashore near the current location of the tunnel at Turtle Bay (around 34th Street on the East River). Having been thrown back during the battle of Brooklyn, he knew he had to bid the Gowanus Creek farewell, and the Marblehead boys used a foggy night and muffled oars to get the entire nascent American army to a place where they could fight without water at their backs. Without these boats and those boaters, he stood the chance of being slaughtered right there on the Brooklyn/Queens boarder. But with an amphibious option (even a retrograde option), he lived to fight another day, and turn things around in the fullness of time by crossing the half-frozen Delaware as a Christmas gift to the Hessian troops holed up in Trenton.

It was also at the start of the Revolutionary War that Americans first fired up their very own Marine Corps. Originally used to fight at sea against other ships, such as shooting down from the rigging and putting boarding parties onto enemy ships to contest ownership with flintlock and cutlass, the Marines quickly became a small and elite unit that was best known for its ability to get ashore and fight without the usually massive logistical backing that a normal army unit would need. There are few stories in military history as inspiring and intrepid as that of the U.S. Marine Corps.

The use of water for attack had many fans in the American Revolution, from John Paul Jones raiding the coast of England (and going ashore) to that ubiquitous visionary, the extremely brave (and later extremely treacherous) Benedict Arnold, who not only launched a bizarre and visionary attack on Quebec by means of a route through darkest Maine that almost any nincompoop would decline, to his building of a fleet and fighting the British with delaying tactics on Lake Champlain. As much as any one man, in his time or any other, Arnold understood how water could be used to take the advantage of a situation in war, and to provide both attacking and retreating options for the imaginative commander. His subsequent traitorous attempt to deliver West Point to the Redcoats is just another example of

Another stylized view, this time of the British forces in 1759 climbing a goat track on the left to get up to the Plains of Abraham, west of Quebec, and then giving battle to the French defenders. The town itself is in the center background. With this tricky move, General Wolfe managed to bamboozle and surprise the French, but neither he nor General Montcalm lived to see the end of the day. But the important thing was that he was able to get his troops ashore in safety.

how well he understood the central role played by waterways, and the strategic importance of that place, dominating the Hudson Highlands there where the river narrows between Storm King Mountain and Breakneck Ridge.

There is also the interesting amphibious case study of the attack on the Iroquois homeland in 1779. Tory-led Indian raids had been devastating to the western frontier, so a multipronged assault was planned, with General John

58

Sullivan coming up from Pennsylvania, and General James Clinton coming down the Susquehanna River from the northeast. Perceiving the river to be too low to float his troops, Clinton cleverly built a dam at Otsego Lake, and then released the captive waters when he wished to shoot down stream and meet with Sullivan. Here was a commander with a deft touch for using water to gain his objective.

Throughout our history, Americans have often showed this kind of prescient understanding of waterways. Troops have been put ashore all over the world beneath our colors. Wisely understanding the Native-American way of traversing the continent, American troops and commanders became adept at forcing their way up and down rivers, and the many tidal creeks of Virginia provided a sort of litmus test for who had the large vision. Often in the Civil War, this was not the commanders with the best political connections, but rather those who knew how to cross and cruise rivers and streams at a relentless pace, who used mobility and obstacles as two sides of the same sword.

But the most daunting operation involving landing an army on a beach was fortunately not an American one, but a combined British-Australian-New Zealand-French affair that was preceded by the fiasco at the Dardanelle's, and followed by the fiasco at Gallipoli in 1915. Winston Churchill had the somewhat clever notion that if he could force a way into the Black Sea he could fall in behind the Central Powers and help out the hapless Russians in the bargain, while helping the "sick man of Europe" (the once mighty and now motheaten Ottoman Empire) into an early grave. The initial landings went all right, and were almost unopposed, but once ashore the troops failed (or rather their leaders failed) to seize the day and press inland at top speed. As a result, thousands of men were trapped either on the beach, exposed to the withering fire of a growing Turkish presence, or slightly inland, engaged in bitter trench battles with those same Turks. The northern beaches, at a place called Anzac Cove, at first pitted thirty thousand men of the British Empire against a mere seven thousand Turks, but once the forward momentum of the amphibious assault was squandered by digging in instead of pressing inland, the mood change can best be summed up by the reporter from *The Times of London* who wrote, "We have landed and dug another graveyard."

The result was a war of attrition that bled the Anzac troops dry, and showed that while Turkey may have been the butt of many jokes, with some German advisors and ambitious young leaders like Mustafa Kemel, they were the equal of any troops in the world, especially when backed up by machine guns.

The shadow of Gallipoli has always fallen like a funeral shroud on any discussion of amphibious options: "We don't want another Gallipoli," was a commonplace expression in the Navy and Marine Corps training and planning of the 1920s and 1930s. Young officers also looked closely at such things as the nature of the beach to be assaulted, and the terrible selection of unseaworthy craft the British had used. To get cannon ashore, often they would have to be slowly rolled up two planks to the bow, and then somehow horsed down two similar planks into the shallows. You can guess how well this went in waves and under fire.

As with so many phases of warfare, World War II was where the Americans first tried and then perfected (as much as such a crap shoot can be perfected) the art and science of

Australian troops led by a British colonel attacking uphill at Gallipoli. The landing went all right at first, but once the Turks got their act together this became one of the pointless blood baths of World War I. Colonel Whiley, shown here, was awarded a posthumous Victoria Cross, and as a result of Gallipoli, the Australians refused to ever serve under the command of a non-Australian general again—to this very day. Gallipoli would be much on the minds of the planners of the Pacific campaign of World War II, and the men of Overlord in Normandy.

thrusting mighty armies onto hostile shores, often against fanatical defenders. The glow of those days almost eclipses the doomsayers who will never forget Gallipoli (such as the Australian generals who refused to ever again be put under someone else's bad plan), in that starting with North Africa in October of 1942, and working through the landings at Sicily and a staggering list of atolls in the Pacific, the Americans became the most studied and successful purveyors of the amphibious assault. Not that they all went without a hitch; evidently the confusion on the African beaches during Operation Torch was enough to worry anyone, and a miscalculation in figuring the tides left hundreds of Marines dead at Tarawa in the Pacific. The same theme kept emerging: to conquer a place by attacking over the beach, you have to first have a good beach—the sand has to be firm enough to land heavy equipment; and there must be ways off that beach.

It was during this time that such specialties as combat swimmers came to the fore, because the need for intelligence about a particular patch of shore was desperately felt, especially after Tarawa. From these early days come the modern-day U.S. Navy SEALs, and from the Marine Raider Battalions come the men of today's USMC Force Recon, the Marines's own recon and combat specialists. Such intelligent men as Willard Bacomb also came to the fore, and his book on beaches, tides, and waves is still just about the last word on the subject. There was also the development of specialty landing craft such as the boats of the Higgins Company of New Orleans, which were boxy affairs that eventually had a ramp in front, and could be driven almost up onto the shore, and then (hopefully) winched off by anchors set (hopefully) not too far out in the surf zone.

The view from a landing craft that had just disgorged its troops on Normandy on D-Day, June 6, 1944. This craft either grounded pretty far out, or else the coxswain refused to go farther ashore. Ahead lie the heavily defended cliffs and ridges of the coast—and the fate of the world hangs in the balance. But by the end of the day, the Americans were well ashore and driving inland, and the end of the Nazi regime was in sight.

These were by no means a paragon of nautical engineering—just look at one next to a clipper ship or skipjack to see what the problems are—but they were just the right boats at just the right time, along with tanks and amtracks that could slosh ashore (sometimes without sinking). It wasn't perfect, but it didn't look like Gallipoli, and it worked from Sicily, Anzio, and Salerno, to Saipan, Iwo Jima, and Okinawa, and on the beaches of Normandy.

The Normandy invasion presented a host of special problems, and is still studied closely for the many lessons that were learned. The gesture was a bold one almost to the point of recklessness; the weather was lousy, and the scale was massive. The beaches were not the best, and were well-defended, but for the first time on such a scale airborne troops were dropped in behind, and the men of the British and American landing parties on Omaha, Utah, Sword, Juno, and Gold beaches showed an intrepid disregard for the desperation of their position. Did men get dropped in the wrong place? Good Lord, yes. But combat leaders on the beach, like General Theodore Roosevelt Jr., figured out pretty quickly where they were, and supposedly simply said, "We'll start the war from right here."

Note that in most of these WWII operations we had control of the sea and control of the sky—an attack by a small group of fast boats or a steady round of dive-bombers could have screwed the pooch on any of these missions. And even with air and sea superiority, these were all close-run operations. It's pretty easy to see why two presidents and almost all of the military leadership thought that trying the atom bomb would be better than exposing American troops and Japanese defenders to a massive amphibious assault on the Japanese home island. The fanatical defense and coconut-log reinforced blockhouses of Iwo Jima didn't incline anyone to push their luck with another strike from the sea.

And yet five years later the flamboyant General Douglas MacArthur, against almost all his advisors, decided to get behind the North Koreans by slamming ashore at Inchon in a daring attack that took advantage of massive tides and the dauntless USMC to hit the left flank of the Korean Peninsula at just the place where we were not expected. In a gamble on a scale with any of the most desperate maneuvers ever undertaken, in ten days his troops had established themselves and were heading north for the Yalu River. Once again, control of the sky and control of the sea aided the attack beyond all knowing.

Later in that decade, the Anglo-French invasion of the Suez Canal heralded one of the most important sea changes in amphibious thinking, as the use of helicopters for the first time on a large scale showed the way of the future. If getting off the beach was close to the be-all and end-all, why not use these chattering eggbeaters to hop and skip like a knight in a chess game over any defenders, and get in behind them to not only discommode their defense, but also begin securing the roads and passages off the beach? As we shall see, this relatively small operation came to have resonant echoes up to today. Be that as it may, the British in the Falklands in 1982 ran a perfectly straightforward and successful landing at Goose Green (pointedly, without any Anzac forces), and small boats took on an entirely new role in Vietnam, where the many fingers of the Mekong River became a new sort of battleground, but this one featuring fast patrol boats of the U.S. Navy, often putting ashore intrepid parties of SEALs.

Today the U.S. military has every strand of this history firmly in mind when they prepare to go ashore somewhere—and interestingly, we prefer not to attack hostile beaches. There are so many other options today that a planner would be considered almost criminally liable were he or she to suggest that we run a WWII-era assault. It would be much more likely in this day and age to use helicopters to get the troops ashore (assuming air superiority), and indeed the USMC has a fleet of helicopter assault ships at the ready which can carry hundreds of men many miles inland without ever getting them wet. They also have the massive LCACs, which is an eighty-foot hovercraft that can go about fifty knots and disgorge men and tanks almost anywhere,

whatever the tide and shore conditions—"No beach out of reach" as they say. And there are even better assault craft now than ever existed before, such as the Advanced Amphibious Assault Vehicle (AAAV, soon to be renamed The Butler), which can not only roll through the surf zone using its hull to ride the waves, but also has a front ramp like the old landing craft. Or else the Marines can stay inside and the darn thing will run like a tank all the way ashore as far as you wish to go—such as the right flank of the recent assault on Baghdad.

Current doctrine calls for an attack about fifty kilometers wide and about thirty kilometers deep, using a mix of over-

A modern-day USMC AAAV is seen here charging hard for the shore, and throwing up quite a wake doing it. It can carry twenty-five men, is defended with a 25mm cannon, and has a top speed of about twenty knots. This is a vast improvement from the old landing craft, in that it can also charge inland after reaching the shore.

the-beach forces and helicopter-borne Marines. The idea is to secure the sky and sea, use speed and surprise to strike where they are least expected, and get about 20,000 Marines ashore in something less than an hour. The less time everybody is exposed, the better. And consider all the things that go into a modern-day amphibious assault, from the SEALs and Force Recon men who come ashore in stealthy small groups (except in Somalia, where they were met by CNN), to the satellite photos, to the air cover provided by the Navy's carrier forces, to the remote sensors put in place to monitor the wind and tide, to the submarines and airplanes making sure that no enemy gets in among the landing craft to foment mayhem at unwelcome times—such as any time after you leave the large ships.

The only reason to attack a beach is to secure a port that is more or less close to that beach. With a port, once you fix the stuff the enemy has blown up or that you wrecked in your assault, you can put troops ashore on any scale you like, and this is widely agreed to be the best way to land armies—not out of little boats or AAAVs or LCACs or helicopters. Once the big troop ships can dock, you just throw down the gangplank and start marching them off the ship, and this can be done (if no one is strafing you) at a mind-boggling pace.

The mighty LCAC, shown in a hard left turn, jammed with men and machines and making for the USS Kersarge during an exercise in 2001. This is why these boys have painted on the side of their hangars "No Beach Out of Reach." It rides on a cushion of air (under that black rubber skirt) and the two giant fans at the back can pivot to make it turn harder than this if need be.

The issue of defending a coast has also been given much thought in the United States, but not seriously enough since World War II, at least until 9/11, and the threat now is unlikely to be a large invasion force coming over the horizon unless al Qaeda has a maritime component that has stayed under the radar. But back in the day, as they say, every major port in the U.S. had its shore defense batteries, such as the endless series around San Francisco, and the ones on either side of the Verrazzano Narrows in New York, or the lonely and abandoned concrete pillboxes of the New

A pretty good shot of a RHIB (rigid hull inflatable boat) being lowered off the starboard side of the USS Juneau, showing the full keel and the inflatable tubes on either side. These are fast and stable craft that can suck up a great deal of abuse, and are favored by Navy SEALs and others whose jobs take them close to hostile shores. Note the powerful radar on a brace over the helmsman, and the calm sea state. Doing this at night in a howling gale would be a little different.

Hampshire coast to guard the Portsmouth Naval Shipyard. These latter emplacements were hardly temporary, using mountains of concrete to shield massive 16-inch guns that broke not a few windows in the neighborhood when they were fired.

In our current age, there has been much debate about the future of amphibious warfare. Will we ever need it again,

69

given how dangerous all such missions are, and the fact that the helicopter has redrawn the battlefield and our notions of mobility and access to the inland portions of hostile countries? Longtime readers of professional journals like the ever-informative "U.S. Naval Institute Proceedings" are always on the lookout for some young lieutenant or retired colonel who is looking to either communicate the end of the amphibious era, or else make yet another impassioned case for the survival of the USMC, despite their specialty being somewhat thrust into the shadows of late. The Marines are reluctant to be folded into any other branch of the service, being already the unwilling stepchildren of the Navy, but at the same time, is there really a justification for having the redundancy of a branch of the service with its own air force, navy, artillery, and air and sea assets? The unsatisfactory but simple answer is "maybe." If you need such troops and such a service, you're not going to want to try to train them in two weeks. And where might we need them? Afghanistan has no coast, and the heavy fighting in Iraq wasn't anywhere near Basra on the Gulf. But given that North Korea is still led by a madman, and that the Chinese really, really would like to fold Taiwan back into their territorial mix, it can be argued that there may be plenty of future operations that require the services of a tough unit like the U.S. Marines. Their dauntless courage and willingness to tackle targets that nobody else would even get close to speak for themselves, and the spirit of the Marines is one of their greatest assets, on a beach or anywhere else. They are used to being shot at, and they are not used to being stopped. How many other units can really make that claim?

Be that as it may, it seems safe to predict that amphibious warfare has a way of cropping up even when historians

*Here's how the USMC hits the beach these days: using amphibious
assault ships like the USS* Belleau Woods *(LHA 3), named for a
legendary Marine battle of World War I. It can disgorge men and
machines at an astounding pace, using LCACs, conventional landing
craft, and helicopters off its deck. The stern is a wet well that can
accommodate small craft and men in safety, and to the port side aft is
an elevator for getting helicopters up to and down from the deck.*

think it is a thing of the past. Certainly after Gallipoli every military planner and thinker went out of their way to figure out how to avoid going in over the beaches—except the visionary men of the USMC, such as Pete Ellis, who evidently foresaw the entire shape of the coming war in the Pacific against Japan, and began laying out in the 1930s what came to be a very costly but ultimately successful series of island-hopping strikes. As to why more of those islands weren't bypassed, history is a mute oracle.

At its best, amphibious operations will always remain a good way to strike an enemy and secure a coast by using brave men to force their way ashore. We have about three divisions of amphibious Marines, somewhere close to 200,000 men, who are trained for and (from what they say) enjoy hostile beach assault, and as such the United States is the world leader in the ability to take a day at the beach to a whole other level. Might they be pressed into the next Korean War? Well, not if there are a lot of nukes involved. Might they be used as shore defense on Taiwan? That depends on how much warning we have and how long it takes China to float her thousands of rickety craft out to the island in question. Will they serve in any clime and conditions you send them to, and do so in a way that covers them with glory and reflects on the highest traditions of the martial arts as fought by brave warriors anywhere throughout history and across the globe? The answer to that one is simple—you bet they will.

CHAPTER 4

Whistling "Garry Owen": Cavalry

IN WARFARE THERE is a continuum of desirable and undesirable ways to operate. Slow, clunky, and feckless would be on one end, and fast, astounding, and hard-hitting would be on the other. And throughout every conflict that we have a record of, the cavalry has always been tight up against the most desirable end of things. While many battles were settled by masses of footmen advancing and grappling with each other, an equal number have been decided by the exceptional mobility and surprising audacity of the cavalry. In our modern age, it is easy to proclaim that everything has changed in warfare, that the uniforms and ways of resolving conflicts are completely new, but this is a shortsighted vision of an activity that is as old as humanity itself. The eternal verities still hold true, and the dash and élan of the cavalry hasn't changed a bit, even though they have retired their horses and now go to war encased in tanks, armored personnel carriers, Hummers, and helicopters. But it's the same old story: mobility is the key to the early stages of any battle, and during the main event the ability to focus a decisive force on an enemy's weak position will always afford an advantage, and in some cases the deciding factor between winning and losing. The cavalry, then and now, has always been an elite and special form of warfare, steeped in tradition and as forward-leaning as any branch of the service can be.

The story of humans making friends with animals is a curious one. Scientists suspect that wild dogs crept in to be near the fire in ancient Asia, and stuck around for handouts. But who was the first person who had the patience and calm demeanor to slowly get close enough to a horse to let the critter be comfortable with him (or her) stroking its mane? Oh, it's easy enough today, after untold generations of interaction, to walk into a field with a bag of apples and pretty soon have every equine unit in sight as a buddy. But somehow (and probably also on those same plains of Asia) some person got it worked out with the local horses that he could not only feed them, but also in time (and in one of the great reckless moves in all of history) actually hop on their backs and attempt to steer them. Those familiar with rodeos can conjure the vision of how this went for the first thousand years. If a horse doesn't wish to travel with you, there are any number of ways he can dispense with his load, from rolling over, to bucking, to galloping swiftly under a low branch.

But the potential gleaned from watching these grass- and hay-driven quadrupeds thundering over the steppes was too good to pass up, despite broken heads and hard words. Horses are intelligent and sometimes fickle creatures, and can actually sense the confidence and control of a good rider. One way to make traveling with them a bit easier is to hitch them to a wagon or chariot, and indeed when Rameses II needed a fast ride at the battle of Kadesh in 1299 BC he got two horses and a chariot to get his bows and spears to the crucial spot and paste the Hittites a good one. Chariots were also used by the ancient Assyrians (of the three horse variety) and by the ancient Celts (who favored one horse and two men, as well as the heads of their enemies festooning their rig like fuzzy dice). The theme is the same as today: get the missile weapons close to the enemy as fast as possible, while also retaining the ability to run away at top speed.

King Cyrus of Persia once discommoded an enemy cavalry unit by confronting them with unfamiliar camels, and elephants have also been used as super-heavy cavalry, one of the downsides being that if they panic they will leave the field with no regard at all for where (or on whom) they are stepping. But let's go back to the intelligent and fickle horse. A horse and rider is always a team effort, and you have to feed and water and rest them. Alexander the Great had his legendary steed Bucephalus, which supposedly only he could mount. Horses are vulnerable to being wounded pretty easily as well as freaking out and bolting around things they don't like, such as fire and snakes. A great deal of training has to go into making a horse fit for war, almost as much as is needed to make men suitable to the maelstrom and carnage of combat.

It is sometimes forgotten today that the first Muslim jihad was a horse-driven campaign that came close to taking over all of Europe, stopped only by Charlemagne. But it was the Huns who really took cavalry to a new level, by using their short sturdy horses and exceptional bow use to confound

As seen here, the Huns were not only ugly and violent, but they also trampled women and children, and seemingly scared even their own horses. This Victorian view shows some of the loathing Europeans developed for these people, but leaves out the exceptional mobility and excellent leadership that enabled them to conquer such vast tracks of land.

and defeat most slow-moving European armies. Attila & Co. were a new sort of army, in that the entire shebang was mounted and mobile, and they were adept at all the classic ruses of warfare, including the fake retreat that can lead to a disorganized enemy rushing into a trap (this never goes out of style), and the so-called "Parthian Shot," which is where you gallop away from your enemy while twisting around and delivering an arrow as you depart. In one of those curious semantic byways beloved of pedants and scribes, the "parting shot" of today's usage would seem to still honor the long-forgotten Parthian.

Of course, when it rains it pours, and the Europeans must have thought themselves singularly cursed when the Mongols showed up in the 1200s. Using the same shaggy ponies that are still for sale in Ulan Bator for a mere $200 a head, the mobile and ferocious forces of Genghis Khan showed a swiftness and savage implacability that swept everything before them. When he conquered the Tartars, he slew every one of them who was taller than a cart axle's height. As a result, he not only united Mongolia, but also swiftly subsumed all the surrounding peoples, and seemingly set his sights on conquering everything from Japan to Iceland. Fortunately, the subsequent leaders of Genghis's people proved less gifted than the first Khan, and as a result Europeans could get back to the business of bashing each other, as well as taking little jaunts to The Promised Land.

Cavalry has always had the same benefits, as well as the same drawbacks. It's expensive and time consuming to be able to afford horses. As a result, only the moderately wealthy could afford to travel and fight on horseback, and thus we have the rise of the knight. Familiar to all of us in some sort of cultural memory, the knight in his glory could bowl over infantry with very little effort, mounted as they were on horses such as those that draw the Budweiser wagons, and decked in a hundred pounds or more of armor. But just as tanks are not invulnerable, neither is cavalry. The British bowmen of Agincourt took an unbelievable toll on the French nobility, who, once they were knocked off their horses became spastic and hobbled targets for even the slowest infantry. Horses could be stopped by pits and trenches dug in the battlefield, and even such devious devices as caltrops, which are four-sided spikes, so designed that no matter how they fall on the ground they will always have one spike up, ready to pierce the unwary hoof. Long lances could also be used to make a sharp hedge that horses would hesitate to be forced through, and sharpened stakes could be emplaced for the same purpose. As late as the battle of Waterloo in 1815, the brave French cavalry was confounded by the British infantry formed in squares with bayonets fixed, and this, combined with the rise of firearms, seemed to spell the end of the proud military horsemen. Yet at the same time, the Napoleonic era was also one of the high points in cavalry history, in that such typically brave and reckless men as Marshal Joachim Murat, the king of Naples, led at one point what may have been the largest cavalry charge of all time—almost 11,000 horsemen at the battle of Jena. The pictures we have of Murat and such beau sabers as the Comte de LaSalle came to stereotype the cavalryman—perhaps not the sharpest tool in the shed, but jaunty and brave to a fault, stylish uniform and perhaps long drooping mustaches, ever willing to gallop headlong and pell-mell into the teeth of an enemy, and believing that most tactical situations could best be resolved by a goodly helping of dash and pluck, combined

At Waterloo, June of 1815, Napoleon waited too long and then threw his cavalry away against a canny opponent. But despite the odds, many of them got in among the British squares and caused what havoc they could, bold and dashing to the last.

with a solid horse and a taste of cold steel. It's a cliché because it so often proved to be quite true. At one point during the Russian Campaign of 1812, eyewitnesses tell us that Murat rode out alone and confronted forty Cossacks (no mean riders themselves) and simply yelled at the astonished enemy until they slunk into the forest.

But for all the gallantry of European cavalry, by the time of the Crimean War and the ill-fated charge of the Light

Confederate cavalry charging at Fairfax Court House on May 31, 1861. This is an accurate portrayal, in that Confederate horsemen preferred pistols and carbines to sabers, and were excellent horsemen. It would be two years before Union cavalry like Stannard's Vermont regiment could truly give them an even fight.

Brigade, anyone with half a brain could see that firearms were outstripping the ability of horses and men to dodge bullets. Meanwhile, in the New World the American cavalry was pursuing their own path. Due to the density of the eastern woodlands, mounted troops played a unique role in the American Revolution. They were most often used in small groups as mounted infantry (with specialized short muskets) and as scouts and spies. And by the time the new Republic got to the Civil War, the proud tradition of the Southern cavalry stepped up to blaze one of the brightest pages in military history. Trained as they were (mostly at West Point) on the campaigns of Napoleon, the Confederate forces initially had a tremendous advantage over their blue-coated opponents. A horse in New England was most often a draft animal for farm work or getting crops to market, or rum out to the farms. But in the South there existed a tradition of chivalry (somewhat at odds with the mean-spirited nature of slavery and racism) that was predicated on every gentleman being a very good horseman. Of course any officer worthy of the title could ride—even the top man, General Robert E. Lee, was able to jump a three-rail fence when hemmed in by Union soldiers at one early battle. He hadn't picked his famous horse, Traveler, for good looks alone.

This meant that when the Civil War started, most any group of Johnny Rebs on horseback supplied their own outstanding mounts, and needed no training in dashing around the landscape with a reckless spirit that Joachim Murat would have applauded. The legendary General J. E. B. Stuart is the paragon of this age, a large and jolly fellow, with a stylish plumed hat and a jaunty cloak, and gathered around him were the finest riders on the best horses the continent had to offer. The exploits of Stuart's men have passed into history, such as their famous ride all the way around the Union army, and while they carried swords proudly, they did most of their fighting with pistols and sawed-off shotguns. And for daring-do, men like John Singleton Mosby and Wade Hampton were not far behind.

During the course of the war, however, it would take more than plucky horsemen to win the day. And cavalry was not without its drawbacks, such as a tendency to gallop off hither and yon just when you most needed them—such as at Gettysburg. By that time also, Union cavalry such as the units under Generals Judson Kilpatrick and Stannard of Vermont were making a name for themselves, as was the youngest brigadier in the army, a long-haired blond named

81

George Armstrong Custer. By the conclusion of the war, the American cavalry had transformed itself into one of the finest and fastest in the world, and that was handy because they were about to be taken to school by perhaps the finest light horsemen to ever gallop across a plain: the Native American Indians.

The Spanish had brought horses with them to Central and South America when they came looking for gold in the 1500s, and the first indigenous peoples they ran across were terrified of the animals. But it wasn't very long before they had stolen a few and gotten the hang of them faster than any people who ever lived. In a mere three hundred years the Native Americans understood the spirit of horses and used them to fight their long losing battle with the white men with a verve and panache unseen since the days of the Mongols, and with some of the same tactics (such as the false retreat and the lightning raid). Tribes as far separated as the Sioux in the north and the Apaches in the south made a point to elevate the horse to the position of a minor god, but from contemporary accounts the Comanche of Texas were the hands-down winners at cavalry warfare. This led in response to the rise of such legendary light cavalry as the Texas Rangers, and made the U.S. Cavalry come up to a mark that would give them a chance when defending the remote forts and pioneer wagon trains of the great Wild West. Without saddles or stirrups, the Comanche could ride like the wind and shoot arrows from under the neck of a galloping horse, something even Murat and Stuart might have balked at trying.

And note the drawbacks of impetuous and reckless caval-rymen: when Custer's Seventh Cavalry made their ill-fated decision to attack a native camp along the Little Big Horn

This Currier & Ives lithograph is called "Custer's Last Charge," and gives some idea of the great esteem that cavalrymen held. Custer was almost a poster boy for armed horsemen, a leader of dash and charisma, the youngest general in the Union army at age twenty-five, known for doing unexpected and daring things—like attacking an enemy of unknown strength in 1876 and getting wiped out down to the last man.

River, probably humming the old drinking song "Garry Owen," the only survivor of the 7th that June afternoon in 1876 was a wounded horse named "Comanche"—still to be seen, stuffed, in the Cavalry Museum in Fort Riley, Kansas.

By the time the 1800s had run their course, the horse was

A French Renault tank plows its way up out of a trench and toward the German lines. The United States was unable to make their own tanks in World War I, and so men like George S. Patton used these French tanks, based on the American Caterpillar tractor, instead. The treads and tracks were pretty good in mud, but it is easy to see why many became stuck and had recourse to chains and cables to get them free.

about to be retired from formal warfare, although old cavalrymen would hear none of it. A young Winston Churchill participated in one of the last charges, at Omdurman in 1898, and young George Patton was a dyed-in-the-wool trooper, designing the last official U.S. cavalry saber, and favoring jodhpurs for most of his life. But the twentieth century would see military horsemen restricted to playing polo because the internal combustion engine was about to sweep everything before it.

Tanks got their start in World War I when the British tried them as a way to end the stalemate on the Western Front, although they broke down a great deal and did not prove to be the answer to that war's muddy problems. It wasn't until the Germans perfected the tactics of the blitzkrieg in the 1930s, and then unleashed it on the world, that the idea of tanks went curiously both backward and forward. Backward, in that the heavy armor of the medieval knights returned, and forward in that the horse was put out to pasture and horsepower in the form of engines powered by gasoline made its entry to the field of battle.

American tanks got their start by borrowing from the French in World War I. Then a Mr. Christie had a bright idea in the 1930s that perhaps a sort of "combat car" would be useful for reconnaissance and scouting work. And while it didn't have much of an engine or any sort of decent gun, the design was taken over by the Russians and emerged as the exceptional T-37, one of the decisive factors on the Eastern Front. Once America was well and truly committed to fighting a world war, it didn't take long for its auto and truck plants to start spitting out tanks that were not as good as the clever and heavy German designs, but made up for this by being produced in numbers beyond all reckoning. Here was where old cavalrymen like George Patton could see the link between the two eras, and used the mobility and firepower of these new tanks to forge a new chapter in special warfare, informed equally by Joachim Murat and the German panzer leader Guderian. But Patton also showed a gift for outrunning his supply lines—perhaps he hadn't studied Custer? And even the mighty German panzers came a cropper on the steppes of Russia, defeated by time and distance and weather on the very terrain that had seen the Huns and Mongols through their early successes, as well as proving to be the graveyard of Napoleon's Grande Armee. This came up as recently as the last war in Iraq, where once again the

The arsenal of democracy in action: here the Chrysler plant is shown in 1944 on a full war footing, putting the treads on an almost complete M3 tank. The M3 weighed 28 tons, could do 25 mph, had a 75mm and a 37mm cannon, as well as four machine guns and a 400hp Wright Whirlwind aircraft engine. It wasn't the best tank of the war, but we made thousands and thousands of them.

tanks and APCs ran too fast and too far, and couldn't always be supplied with mechanics or fuel as well as they might have been. But that's always been a trade-off of speed in warfare: if you rush forward as fast as you can you may well surprise your enemy and achieve an early success, only to look back and not see your people there behind you.

Curiously, by the time of Vietnam the concept of cavalry had taken on an entirely new meaning, in that helicopters were now part of the tactical mix, and even styled themselves as "Air Cav," complete with crossed saber insignia and hats with tassels of a kind Custer would have recognized. Commanders could now move troops and gear around the field in ways that had never been tried before, and "air mobility" became a central tenet of modern warfare. It was as if horses became as large as small boats and could fly—the possibilities seemed endless, and in places

The mighty C-130 is shown here supporting the First Cavalry Division one day in 1966, flying troops back from An Khe to Bam Bleh, Vietnam. Such mobility is still a large part of modern cavalry planning, and the C-130 is still with us, and hopefully will be for many years. Note the huge tail for stability and control.

where tanks lost much of their utility (such as Vietnam and Afghanistan), the Air Cav, while not a war-winning development, could still pull off astonishing maneuvers that would have warmed the heart of any cavalryman.

Today's cavalry is a decisive arm that can in its American incarnation sweep anything before it—anything, that is, that cares to stay and fight a tank and helicopter battle. Tanks are great at fighting the sort of war they are designed

87

to fight, and today's American armor and helicopters have no real equal anywhere in the world. This does not mean they cannot be defeated, and sometimes in remarkably prosaic ways. The mighty M1A1 (and M1A2) main battle tank is probably the best armored vehicle ever built, with its Chobham reactive armor (which hopefully blows out before an incoming missile can blow it in) and its massive 120mm main gun. It is sixty-three tons of attitude that can go 42 mph and do that for 289 miles, bumping over obstacles (as long as they are not more than about four feet high), capable of blowing away any other tank on earth.

But you have to see tanks as part of the overall battle plan: once the air force and artillery have softened things up, the M1A1s roll forward, backed up by Bradley Fighting Vehicles (or the old M113 if you're the last one to the APC pool on the morning of the battle) with their 25mm guns and troops inside, and behind them the wreckers and mechanics and fuel trucks. At the same time troop and gunship helicopters are making their play up and over the enemy, and it is hoped that all these factors, reminiscent as they are of elements of traditional cavalry warfare, will come together and provide you with not only Special Forces and airborne and helicopter assault troops behind and among the enemy, but then a massive armored assault at the front door that will give the enemy no choice but to hang it up. But that's on the sand tables at Sandhurst and West Point and St. Cyr.

Hardly anything goes as well as it might in the real world, and this goes double for fighting wars. It takes forever to get tanks anyplace on the globe, because their 63-ton bulk just doesn't fit in most normal airplanes—excellent ports and large ships are needed, as well as a good deal of lead time to place them where you'd like them. Tanks are not known for their stealth, being voted "weapon least like a jaguar dropping out of a tree." They can literally be heard coming for miles and miles. And that 43 mph number is top speed on the Autobahn—but you shouldn't count on an advance of much more than five miles an hour once the shooting starts, and perhaps much slower. Tanks have to be protected, which seems like a wacky notion given the fact that they are the baddest motor scooters on the planet, but consider that good sharpshooters can blow the antennas off a tank without too much trouble. There's also the "see and be seen" factor: when you're all worried in a tank about things like shells and chemicals, you naturally hunker down and button 'er up—thereby greatly restricting your ability to see what the threat is and where it is coming from. But if you get curious and pop up out of your hatch, the same fella who shot the antenna off can take you under fire without too much trouble. The average tank commander is, after all, wider than an antenna.

If you drive a tank recklessly a tread can be thrown, and that would mean a long period of forced inaction where you are essentially a fixed gun while the crew tries to get the tread back on. And even more than the car in your drive-way, every system and part of a tank has to be finessed and maintained at all times, because each one is of vital importance in battle. A laissez faire approach to mechanical issues in armored warfare is a recipe for disaster.

Tanks cannot and should not operate alone, although sometimes parking them in a bad part of town is useful as a reminder to the locals about who the new sheriff is and what he can do if he's unhappy. Tanks need to function with a logistical supply unit nearby (and these units are prone to

being chewed up because most of what they carry is fuel and ammunition), and with other tanks, air cover, and infantry working in coordination to achieve their goals. Depending on the needs of the battlefield, tanks will travel in a line with their guns swung out to port and starboard, and a tank on point and one on drag at the rear, or else in a line abreast. If the terrain can be exploited it will be by clever and experienced tankers, such as using the "bounding overmatch," where one tank or section goes ahead and gets in a position to cover the advance of the other half of the unit.

American tanks also sometimes operate as a three-tank patrol, with a lead tank being covered by the other two; and for defense they can also dig tanks in (sacrificing mobility for the security of a hole) and hide them in buildings or among shrubbery of a suitable density, enabling them to get

An armored column of American vehicles moves through the tense streets of Baghdad on their way to secure a market. You can't win a guerilla war using tanks, and such columns have proven to be irresistible targets for roadside bombs and RPGs. Many tank units in Iraq have found themselves dismounting and patrolling on foot, because it is easier and safer than driving around like this.

off the first, often decisive, shot. But today's world features so many great antitank rockets that they need to keep an eye out for any infantry that seems like it is stealthing up on their position instead of fleeing in terror as it ought. And for that they can't be buttoned up—they have to be out of their hatch and looking around, although modern sensors are a great help in identifying things like warm bodies on a battlefield.

When American tanks have a good target, such as the foolish attackers and terrified retreating forces of the first Iraq War in 1991, they can simply go to town and put everything before them to the sword so fast the enemy won't even notice they have just lost the majority of their armor and trucks in a series of fireballs. And if the terrain is right (such as in Iraq or anywhere where there is a lot of pretty flat land) the advance of a modern armor battalion (about fifty-four tanks) is a wonder to behold. Keep in mind the difficulties with outrunning the fuel and mechanics, however. In the present Iraq war, the speed of the assault, always such a desirable feature of military operations, in some ways backfired in that the tanks were often halted for lack of fuel and fix up breaks, and there really wasn't that much opposition of the kind that tanks most like to see. Most of the Iraq army melted away, taking their weapons with them, and for many months after we were treated to a seminar concerning what tanks are not good at: containing a rebellious populace, fighting a guerilla war, or responding to hit-and-run strikes by religious zealots shielded by civilians. There are also reports that at least one strange weapon was used against our tanks in the form of some sort of concentrated plasma beam, and while this hasn't been confirmed, it would mean that there's yet another vulnerability waiting to be studied at the staff college before we next try to use tanks to accomplish our national aims. Many of the tanker units deployed found themselves dismounting and brushing up on their infantry patroling skills, because that was the only way to negotiate the narrow streets and hostile peoples of the Tigris and Euphrates. It took months for them to be replaced with MPs and others trained for what was as far from an armored war as can be imagined. As to why the planners had failed to see that the speed of the assault would outstrip the support units, or that military forces other than tanks would be needed for months (and perhaps years) afterward, there hasn't been any rush to accountability.

Does this mean that the day of the tanks is over? That next to the stuffed figure of "Comanche" at Fort Riley will be an Abrams main battle tank, as a relic of the way things used to be? Hardly. It is very hard to foresee future conflicts, but something tells us there will still be the need for a clanking behemoth that can shoot its way in anywhere, and whose rumble will warn mere infantry to steer clear. Used correctly, and on the right terrain, and given enough fuel and mechanical back up, American armor will always have an edge in that it is the largest and most sophisticated tank force ever fielded. We should watch out for a few things,

Of course, cavalry today means more than horses and tanks. These are U.S. Army OH-58D Kiowa Warrior helicopters parked at Rhein Main Air Base in Germany, about to be loaded up in 1996 to go to Bosnia. They are part of the 4th Aviation Brigade Cavalry Unit. These are two-seater scout choppers with all manner of gee-whiz technology, as indicated by the black balls above the rotors, which house low-light image sensors, laser range finders, thermal imaging, and television cameras to broadcast the battlefield back to the commanders.

such as the new Chinese attack helicopter, which is surmised to be especially designed as a tank buster, and the rise of new weapons such as the plasma beam. The United States hasn't faced an aerial threat in a long time, and we have no real idea of what a swarm of enemy helicopters would mean in terms of changes to our tank tactics.

The essential idea of cavalry will never go out of style, because it will always be a good idea to move fast and hit hard, and at this task tanks and helicopters excel within their limitations. The ability to do a fast reconnaissance and then follow it up with a rapid assault and even a massive strike will always be a good idea, and that goes for any number of future scenarios just as it has proven true in the past. For this reason it seems safe to say that tanks and Air Cav will be with us for quite a while. Then, of course, there was the astounding footage from Afghanistan in the fall of 2001, when Special Forces troopers attached to the Northern Alliance were shown briefly riding into combat on actual horses. That was what the locals were using for mobility in a harsh land, and that's what the Delta Force, CIA, SEALs, and Green Beret warriors were using as well. They hadn't shaved since they had dropped in to whack the Taliban, and so had a good start on their drooping mustaches, and with their M4 carbines it didn't look as if they missed the old sabers at all. There was one American soldier who had obviously grown up on a ranch in Wyoming and appeared to be having a fine old time, and then another fellow who looked like he was Larry from Flatbush, stuck atop a steed whose name translated from Pashto into "Diablo" or "Dynamite," and you could tell it was going harder for him—but in the great tradition of the U.S. Cavalry, he was getting the hang of it. Maybe not whistling "Garry Owen" just yet, but definitely riding to the sound of the guns.

CHAPTER 5

Whispering Death: Snipers

FAR REMOVED FROM the staid precincts of policymakers and think tanks, perched on a high point or dressed as a bush, snipers are the sharp sting of modern infantry. It is their job to move from friendly positions into hostile territory, usually in pairs of shooters and spotters, and to make their way forward until they can assess the enemy position and take a shot (or several) that will have an effect out of all proportion to the cost of the ammunition involved. Because while an ordinary soldier might go through several magazines of ammo while defending or attacking a position, sometimes just to "keep the enemy's head down," the sniper's job is to make sure that whatever the range and whatever the target, their first shot will result in either a dead enemy soldier or a wrecked piece of expensive equipment, as well as throwing the other side into disagreeable confusion and fear. This is a job for someone with drive, discipline, determination, patience, cold-blooded resolve, and field craft well beyond the average recruit.

Given how good snipers are at what they do and how much enthusiasm they bring to their work, it can seem like cold-blooded murder when they pull the trigger. This accounts for some of the traditional misunderstanding and outright loathing that they have triggered in people's minds over the years. But here is a good place to begin the discussion of what snipers are and what they do. Under the laws of modern warfare—and yes, there is an entire legal field devoted to the rules of this institutional mayhem that we call war—once the fuse is lit and war is declared, people wearing the uniform of the enemy can be shot from whatever distance you care to engage them at—and that includes more than a mile away with a .50-caliber rifle and the best scope you can afford. As to how this pertains in situations where war has not been declared, or in law enforcement when police snipers take on hostage-takers and violent criminals, there is a gray area, but it is connected to military sniping, in that the general thinking is that shooting one person may well save the lives of many others.

Something along these lines was behind the colonial British method of crowd control in places like India, where, when a hostile mob gathered, often a British officer would go to confront them with one rifleman. Surveying the loudest and most vocal of the hostiles, legend has it that he would say to his corporal: "Shoot that man," (no doubt indicating his choice with a swagger stick), and more often than not the dropping in his tracks of a particularly vociferous individual would have an immediate calming effect on the rest of the gang. Such selective culling is no longer used with civilian crowds—just another benefit of embedded journalists and their omnipresent cameras.

Be that as it may, the judicious killing of selected targets and/or the destruction of high-ticket military equipment on the battlefield has much the same effect upon an enemy as it ever did: they can no longer focus on their own affairs and just schlep around doing whatever they are trying to do. Now they have a very real and tangible problem, in that there are snipers among them, and whispering death is lurking at their shoulder with every step. Hardly any units are so well trained as to simply shrug it off when commanders and radiomen start dropping around them, and their fuel and helicopters start exploding for seemingly no reason on a bright sunny morning.

In this way sniping is somewhat akin to that moment in chess when a bishop, rook, or queen suddenly shatters the protective back row of the chess board and shoots across many squares to eliminate a piece you had previously thought to be safe. There is surprise, and regret, as well as an all-out attempt to punish the intruding piece, and a wary vigilance lest there come future unwelcome shocks to your rear areas. Snipers are well aware of this effect, and their selfless dedication to their art can be said to approach a certain gleeful enjoyment of the stealth and shock on which their chosen field is predicated. It's just human nature, really. Snipers happen to deal in accurate, precise, and long-range death in a way that cannot be sugarcoated, and they operate with a mindset that most civilians (thankfully) must struggle to understand. In another realm, this is the guy you want doing the most finicky safety work on your car, and making sure that every damn inch of all the miles of electrical cable in a jumbo jet are inspected for wear and shorts before you take your vacation to Disneyland.

To be a sniper you have to not only master the entire range of infantry skills, such as living and moving in the field in all terrain and every weather condition and time of day and night, but you also need intelligence far above the average, to have spent immense amounts of time firing all sorts of weapons, a cunning and wise ability to get where you are not expected, the ability to shrug off the fact that you're exposed and behind the lines (usually), forget that you're tired, cold/hot, hungry, scared and/or not feeling well, and line up to take what is expected to be, in the sniper's catch phrase, "one shot, one kill." The fact that a person is going to die in your plain view and because of your actions has to be shunted to one side, and the very real possibility that his friends will soon come looking for you with no intention of capture and interrogation, or anything other than returning to their base with your head on a pole, also must be swept to one side. Because if you hit the right person, or piece of gear, you may accomplish things like completely blunting an enemy offensive, or even finishing a war—and all for the cost of one bullet, as well as years of training.

Historically snipers had to wait for firearms to be developed with enough accuracy for any kind of sharpshooting, because early guns had no reliable lethal ability much beyond eighty yards. Even so, one is tempted to troll through the ages and point to examples such as the slaying of King Harold by an arrow through the eye at the battle of Hastings in 1066, which happened near the end of the battle, but nevertheless made his entire army dissolve around his corpse. It is not thought that this was an aimed shot, however; as the Norman archers (like many early bowmen with indifferent equipment and accuracy) seemed to specialize in throwing clouds of arrows into the air in the hope that the resulting plunging fire would hit something useful if it persisted in raining down on the other army.

Hunters were the first armed men to give some thought to the accurate use of weapons, and their connection to sniping is still a clear and vital one. Early hunters had much more than sport in mind, as a failure in the field meant another night of mush at home, or outright starvation. Early rifles such as flintlocks were also time-consuming to load, making a follow-up shot unlikely for all but the most lethargic game. Native-American bow hunters (as well as primitive peoples worldwide, from Siberia to the Amazon) did not make trick shots at a thousand yards. They were known for being able to get close to animals that were wary and skittish, and then deliver without fail a shot that would not let the animal run off into the bush merely wounded, but instead drop like a stone and die as quickly as possible. By the time of the American Revolution, rifled muskets reached their zenith in both manufacture and use by woodsmen on the rebel side, and groups such as Morgan's Riflemen developed a fine reputation (as well as British loathing) for their ability to spot officers (not hard, as they were not carrying rifles, often dressed up real pretty, and might even have been riding a horse and carrying a map and telescope, as if to say: "Shoot me!") and drop them in battle. The results were often far beyond the effort expended. The shooting of a British officer named General Simon Fraser Tim Murphy of Morgan's men at three hundred yards at the battle of Saratoga is often pointed to as an example of what snipers could do in the field to aid an army hardpressed in battle.

The idea of rifling had been around for a long time, in that it was discovered that a spinning bullet had more range

An American sniper in the Revolutionary War dispatches two unlucky British lobsterbacks. Now, given that sixty seconds is fast for reloading a flintlock, especially while entwined in a tree branch, did the second fellow wait for a minute or more after his mate clutched his head and fell down?

100

and accuracy than a simple round shot pushed out the front by black powder. By cutting a series of spiral grooves into the inside of a gun barrel, spin could be imparted, much the same as a well-thrown football, and the resulting shot would carry farther and hit closer to what the primitive sights were aimed at by their user. But this took a lot of time and training, and rifles were slower to reload than the simple musket, which has a bore that is larger than the bullet, allowing for ease of loading (along with lack of much accuracy, because the ball would ricochet from side to side after the trigger was pulled, making shooting quite a gamble as to whether the bullet would be anywhere near the aiming point). Sights were sometimes as simple as a bead or blade grafted onto the front, and while this did indicate the danger zone out ahead of the shooter, you could hardly drive tacks with it.

Interestingly, Swiss and German immigrants to the backwoods of Pennsylvania brought with them the finely made rifles from their homeland, and a culture of accurate shooting that took the form of contests and impromptu shootarounds, and it was there that the so-called Pennsylvania Rifle made its appearance. By the time of the War of 1812, due to western expansion, many of them had moved a bit farther from the eastern seaboard, and the rifle became fixed in the public's mind as the Kentucky Rifle, examples of which can still be purchased today. With a long barrel and an elegant stock, sometimes of tiger-stripe maple, these early rifles came in everything from .32-caliber up to .45 or .50, far less than the average .70-caliber muskets that the average soldier was issued. The squirrel hunters and marksmen of the American wilderness had an efficient and legendary ability to use just one shot to drop almost anything they came across, from hostile locals to panthers, not to mention the nervous and nimble whitetail deer. In their hunting, almost none of the game animals stood still for any amount of time, except for the lugubrious turkey; the rest of the wildlife had a tendency to make a series of jerky moves while they fed, always on the alert and ready to bolt. As a result, shots had to be lined up and taken with a deft surety that only great experience could foster in the average human. When this translated to warfare, American hunters-turned-soldiers established a reputation for fancy shooting that has endured to this day.

It was also during the American Revolution that a Scotsman named Ferguson not only invented his own breech-loading rifle, but also got permission to organize a small corps of men armed with his invention. For some reason, it never took off, and Ferguson getting wounded didn't help. There was probably the traditional loathing inherent in Special Forces, not to mention the opinion most regular soldiers have had of snipers as mere assassins and murderers. Interestingly, Ferguson once had the chance to shoot George Washington in the field, and desisted because Washington turned and rode away, and he didn't fancy popping the great man in the back. This brings to mind the story related by George Orwell concerning his service fighting the fascist forces of General Franco in the Spanish Civil War of the 1930s. Orwell, of course, was a writer and intellectual, but he loathed fascism, and so volunteered to serve in the field. One day in the trenches he spotted an enemy soldier exposed across the way and lined up his rifle for a shot, only to desist when he saw that the other guy was relieving himself. Orwell did manage to kill a few men during his service, but he also passed up other shots. Oddly there is

This is the trigger group of a breach-loading flintlock rifle designed by Major Patrick Ferguson, a rare and valuable antique, especially as the serial number of this one is "2." The handle on the left rotates the entire trigger guard, exposing the breach for loading. Ferguson was a clever man, but unlucky in battle. A sniper himself during the American Revolution, he was in command at King's Mountain, where an American sniper put the kibosh on his life of inventions at the height of the battle, causing the leaderless British troops to surrender.

entire literature of shots not taken that is almost as interesting as the shots that have been taken. Would Orwell have shot General Franco, even if he were going to the bathroom? Yes, probably, and even if he had turned his back. Eighteenth-century niceties had been mostly swept away by the time of the bitter struggle in Iberia in the twentieth century.

The British did come to recognize the value of the rifleman in their time fighting the French in Spain, and regiments like the 95th Rifles became legendary for their use of long-range and deadly technology to speed up conflicts by judicious shooting. And a French marksman in the mast of a ship managed to kill Admiral Horatio Nelson, the legendary one-arm/one-eye genius of British naval legend during a close encounter. Nelson had insisted on wearing his most gaudy uniform—a form of suicide that few would repeat as accuracy improved. Those early rifles also had no socket for a bayonet, and riflemen often didn't do as well in the field as the more stolid musket brigades, who were content to simply level one or three hundred guns and blaze away before the time came for cold steel. But sharpshooters were rightly seen as scouts as well as shooters, and in this time we have the very beginnings of fieldcraft as we know it today, based on hunting methods and the stealthy offensive actions of the American Indians. The 95th Rifles were well known as skirmishers (light infantry) who could not only probe an enemy position, but also kill French officers and artillerymen at a cracking pace. Why bang a drum and blow a bugle when you can slink in on your belly and get the lowdown on the enemy without their knowing it, and maybe even shoot their captain as long as you're there? As to whether this was "gentlemanly," well, gentlemen thought not, and snipers thought it was a fine idea. The two categories didn't often overlap.

With the development of the rifle to include faster loading, better manufacture, and more stable ammunition than a dollop of powder, a patch, and a ball, by the time of the American Civil War the Yanks and Rebs had done a great deal of target work and hunting, and there was a culture of fast, accurate shooting that only grew as it was seen how effective it could be. By then rifles had been improved by precise manufacture to the point that targets were killed at ranges exceeding one thousand yards, included General John Sedgwick, who had just lambasted his men for ducking from the sound of bullets when he was fatally struck. He

A close-up detail from Winslow Homer's excellent engraving of a Union sharpshooter. He is using a Sharps rifle with an early telescopic sight, and is wedged in the crotch of a tree. Snipers on both sides of the Civil War had great success at increasingly long ranges, although a tree is not considered a good sniper perch in modern doctrine—it cuts down on the chance to "shoot and scoot."

had claimed they couldn't hit an elephant at that range, but the Confederates weren't out for elephants that day.

The Civil War was also the first time that snipers dueled with one another, and this will come up later as one of the prime directives of the modern sniper: to kill others of his ilk wearing the wrong uniform. There is an account of a Union position taking rifle fire from somewhere close, so they put a cap on a stick and raised it over the ramparts (this never goes out of style). The Johnny Reb shot, and the Bluecoats placed a ramrod in the hole the bullet made in the back wall, and thus discovered by sighting along the ramrod that their enemy was in a tall elm tree one hundred yards away. They quickly peppered the top of the tree, and their troubles for that day came to a grinding halt. This also brings up the subject of trees and church steeples, which seem like such a great place to hide and shoot from, but are in reality death traps, as once you are spotted there is no graceful exit possible. The first telescopic sights also made their appearance in the 1860s, as well as rifles like the .52-caliber Sharps, which was breech-loaded and accurate enough for some pretty fancy shooting. The Sharps later swept the Plains of buffalo with as little problem as it had with Native Americans, and a small group armed with the Sharps was almost invulnerable to repeated enemy attacks, as was proven at two sharp little battles ten years apart in the Wild West. The Spenser and Henry rifles also came onto the scene, and were tried by units like Berdan's Sharpshooters, but the Sharps was the long arm of choice.

In the Second Boer War fought from 1899 to 1901, the Boers with their Mauser rifles put on rather a seminar that had at least two tangible results: the adoption of khaki for a uniform color that didn't shout out "Shoot me!" and the sudden emphasis on marksmanship that swept through the British army. By World War I, British soldiers had a fine and accurate rifle in the .303 Enfield, with a ten-shot clip and a bolt action. Big-game hunters in Africa and India, such as Sir Samuel Baker, had also done a great deal of work on rifles and shooting against the most dangerous game (besides man)—the lion, tiger, leopard, rhino, elephant, and worst of all, the Cape buffalo. Once any of these critters got it in their heads that you meant them harm, they took personal and extreme umbrage with your choice of sport and came for you with unstoppable fury—especially the Cape buffalo. With the boss of his horns lowered and fire coming from his nostrils, hunters found that only a fast shot up the

106

nostril had any chance of reaching the tiny enraged mind of these creatures. Those early African hunting guns were the legendary "twin rifles," being a rifle with two barrels side by side like a sporting shotgun, and in calibers up to an inch—which is a mighty big rifle. This was considered the safest way to get two good fast shots at game who would reduce you to a grease stain on the veldt if they could reach you. Experienced hunters also carried the next two cartridges between the second, third, and fourth fingers of the right hand, ready to open the breech, eject the spent shells, and slam home the next two before snapping the gun shut and seeing how close the rhino had gotten.

But when Mauser came up with their almost bombproof bolt-action design, it changed not only hunting but warfare as well, and once the Boers demonstrated to the British that they could, by long practice and a bad attitude toward outside meddlers, slay anything they could see, not only could dangerous game be shot from a much safer distance, but also the ground was laid for the first really efficient use of snipers on the Western Front in World War I. In that sorry conflict, snipers came to the fore, being trained in actual schools instead of just picking the best shot in the company for some tricky shooting, and they used things like metal plates to hide behind, and even elaborate fake trees to hide within and strike without warning. Of course the fact that most of the trees had been cut down by shell fire and machine guns did make this stunt a short-lived one, nevertheless it took a few people by surprise. A legendary big-game hunter named Major Hesketh-Pritchard started the first scout/sniper school for the British, and before the end of the war every major combatant had some type of such training going for them.

There were still Americans who came to the colors with a pretty good idea of how to shoot things in the woods, such as Sergeant Alvin York of Tennessee. Originally a Quaker and objector to the war, his legendary exploits have received the full Hollywood treatment by Gary Cooper, but the actual record is more amazing still. Basically, when cut off from his company, York had a short and sharp tussle with some Germans, and convinced more than a hundred that it was better to surrender to him than try to out shoot his deadly eye. At one point, when rushed by a squad in line, he used an old hunting trick and knocked them off one at a time—from the rear. But the well-known story of Sergeant York should be balanced by the deadly achievements of a Native-American soldier who arrived with the AEF and scored fifty-eight kills. Perhaps a movie will be made someday about Private North-West Wind.

The Germans were not without their own fine shooters, many of them huntsmen from dark forests, and indeed the word "sniper" is said to come from the Germans. It is reported that some sectors of the British trenches lost one hundred men a day to precise German shooting with finely made telescopic sights. The use of decoys and snipers fighting snipers flourished in those muddy trenches, but snipers on one's own side had to even deal with the label of "assassin" and the feeling that they were somehow introducing an underhanded and tawdry element to warfare—as if such a thing were possible. It rather reminds one of the saying "You can no more win a war than you can win an earthquake." But due to this perception, the various sniper schools were stood down at the end of hostilities in 1918; this despite the fact that a great deal of intelligence had been gathered by snipers due to their training in observation and

A U.S. Marine in battle in the Pacific during WWII takes aim with his Thompson submachine gun. Note that this is the later version with the cocking handle on the right side, no compensator on the muzzle, and a 20-shot clip. While hardly a sniper's first choice, it does point out the emphasis on marksmanship in the USMC, where everyone from the cooks to the top general are expected to be riflemen if the situation calls for it. As such, this man is aiming carefully, and because the Thompson climbs up and to the right, you start at the bottom left of a target and let it work through naturally. Note also the .45 Colt in a shoulder holster, and the old-fashioned puttees, now called gaiters.

the close scrutiny they habitually paid anything within their field of fire.

As with so many of the military arts, World War II proved to be a watershed for sniping, and all sides produced shooters on a scale and of an ability unheard of before the war. German snipers took top honors for equipment in both rifles and optics, and the Japanese seem to have been at the bottom of the barrel in terms of training and long-term effectiveness, but even so the effect of snipers on Okinawa and Iwo Jima was palpable and most unwelcome. Even if they only got one shot off before being hosed out of a tree by a BAR, the Japanese managed to kill quite a few officers such as Andrew A. "Ack Ack" Haldane, USMC, and his loss was described as the worst his company suffered in the entire Pacific campaign—a grim tribute to what even amateur snipers could accomplish.

It was also during this time that one of the great sniper legends grew, that of the duel between the Russian Vassili Zaitsev and the head of the German Sniper School, Major Konings. The story seems to owe more to Stalin's propaganda than reality, but supposedly Zaitsev was so effective amidst the rubble of Stalingrad that the Nazis sent their best

A Russian woman sniper using a Mosin Nagant rifle in a posed shot. In combat she would have much better cover, wouldn't have a shiny device on her cap, and would have a more professional grip on her rifle—both hands are wrong in this shot, too far back, and too tentative. The rifle also doesn't seem as if it is tucked into her shoulder correctly—when this goes off, it will hurt. Be that as it may, there were many Russian women in combat, especially as pilots, and quite a few snipers. Russian snipers were among the best in the world, both at shooting and acting as scouts.

man after him, and after a cat and mouse game of several days Zaitsev popped Konings—right through his telescopic sight if you're inclined to learn your history from the cinema. Whatever the actual story, in this episode we can see the beginnings of the modern sniper's lore and legend: he's a ghost, moving through the shattered battlefield on a deadly and personal mission, and he has the patience of a mountain cat, waiting, waiting, for just the right moment, to take just the right shot, and with one bullet kill just the right person. It was also in World War II that the Germans perfected the sniper ambush, which is when three shooters are placed in a triangulated position so that anything that enters the "kill box" will never leave it. Also, effective silencers came into use, and the best of them, such as the British DeLisle carbine, used a subsonic .45 round to make the loudest sound of their operation the working of the bolt.

The United States Marine Corps also began its climb to the top of the sniper ladder, a position that they arguably hold to this day. Marines have always had an intimate and needful relationship with their rifles, and they still pride themselves that everyone from the cooks to the commandant of the Corps can pick up any rifle and become a deadly marksman should the need arise. In Korea and Vietnam they were still using the old Springfield 30-06 bolt-action rifle of 1903, and many of the old-timers swore by it. After all, it was good enough for Sergeant York and Private North-West Wind, and that's pretty good company for shooters. There was even a .50-caliber M2 heavy machine gun that was rigged with a telescopic sight and had some good success in Vietnam, but mostly the snipers coming from the new schools in America used a Remington or Winchester rifle in about .300 caliber, and they had amazing success in a confused war conducted in terrible terrain. But it was perfect sniper country—lots of cover, and all the night and rain and fog anyone could want. The only real problem was the failure of the enemy officers to clump together as often as American snipers wished they would.

Today there are American snipers that are integral parts of every unit that does specialized warfare, including Delta, Navy SEALs, Army Special Forces, Marine Force Recon, USAF Special Operations, and the CIA's growing paramilitary wing—who are mostly ex-Special Forces anyway. We deploy snipers wherever and whenever we deploy more standard military units, and they are used in both war and police matters a great deal more often than anyone is aware. The modern USMC shoots the M40A1 (and its A2 and A3 variants), that being a version of the Remington 700-series rifle, chambered in NATO 7.62X51mm. It weighs fourteen and a half pounds, which is heavy, has a five-round magazine that slips into the bottom of the receiver, and a heavy barrel for accuracy that is 24-inches long and has four grooves in a right-hand twist. The bullet travels at 2,540 feet per second, which covers a lot of ground in a short amount of time. Anyone you hit with this will go down, as opposed to the Barrett Light Fifty, which is a .50-caliber rifle in both bolt action and semiautomatic that will vaporize anything it hits. The Barrett is overkill for counter-sniper work, but is the bomb when it comes time to destroy trucks, light armor, jeeps, and even Scud missiles on their launchers, at which tasks it excels. It can destroy helicopters and ventilate defensive positions pretty much without fail, and when the IRA got a hold of it the Barrett became a weapon of terror—which role it may take on again. The British countered its

The new M-40A3 sniper rifle now being phased into the Marine Corps. Note the heavy barrel for accuracy, the space-age plastic furniture of the stock, the steep comb of the grip, and the spacers to adjust the stock length to accommodate a wide variety of body sizes. The bipod can be unscrewed, if so desired, but otherwise it is a steady and not too cumbersome rest for the weapon.

use in Northern Ireland with their best SAS and Royal Marine snipers, and the problem went away.

Sniper selection for the United States military takes its cue from the Royal Marines, and is as rigorous and demanding as any training available anywhere in the world today. Men don't usually get thrown out of sniper school— they resign themselves. It's pretty clear to the instructors who can cut it and who cannot. Candidates must be expert infantrymen with a broadbased knowledge of every arcane pursuit on the modern battlefield, from command and control to how the food is brought up, because they will be asked to sneak behind the enemy lines, understand everything they see, shoot the most important people and stuff, and get back to report the important intelligence. Training starts with things like observation. For instance, they draw

113

a grid with six sides, place common objects on the grid, and give the would-be sniper one minute to look at the pattern. Then they have them run a mile and do one hundred push ups, and ask them about the grid. Most normal folks will fail to run the mile, throw up doing twenty push ups, and have forgotten all about the grid.

Then there is the eternal question of range. You cannot shoot accurately if you do not know how far away your target is, and as a result the estimation of range goes back at least to the time of the American Revolution. There are some handy benchmarks, such as when a man's face is discernable (not much beyond 150 yards), the windows on a

A USMC sniper doing his best "Yup, just a bush!" impression, although his rifle is pretty obvious. You can easily make out the barrel, telescopic sight, and bipod under the barrel. There are some things you can do to disguise this, but you don't want to mess with anything that will compromise the accuracy of the weapon. But he has certainly done a fine job of breaking up his silhouette and blending his body in with the terrain upon which he is operating.

house can be seen (not much more than a mile), but basically they have to practice and keep practicing to get it so they can glance at things and say "about 300 yards." But if they do they fail, because nothing in the sniper's world falls into the category of "about."

Modern snipers are masters of camouflage and concealment, using every fold of the earth and piece of shrubbery to hide in and around. They also have "ghillie suits" (named for the Scots gamekeepers and poachers tactics of blending in), which enable them to become part of the landscape. What you do is take a good look at where you will be operating, and then construct an all-over garment that replicates most of the features of that landscape, be it sage brush or green leaves, using both fabric strips and natural materials. The key here is to break up the outline so that all the subtle clues that scream "man with a gun!" do not get transmitted to your target. Anecdotal evidence is that such wily hunters as the Comanche tribe used this against buffalo, getting off their horses and walking toward the buffalos on the far side of their pony—on the theory that buffalo cannot or are unwilling to count legs. Interestingly, there is some anecdotal evidence from Canada that bears and wolves know the

First used by poachers and gamekeepers in Scotland, the so-called ghillie suit comprises strips of suitably colored fabric stuck on a jacket. At their best, they produce an amorphous shape that doesn't resemble a man, and blends into the landscape almost imperceptibly—just the way snipers like things to be.

difference between tasty and unarmed humans, and "bad guy with a thunder stick." Some of that same thinking is still with the snipers, in that they soften and blend all their edges (like helmets, rifles, arms, and legs) into a unified whole that says: "I'm a bush. Yup, just a bush. No worries here, mate!" You have to see these guys do this to believe how well they blend in, and what a shock it is when they move.

Snipers usually work in pairs, both of whom are sniper-qualified, but one is the shooter and the other is the spotter. This helps with defensive tasks, as well as being more social than solo work. There are still a few "lone wolves,"—legendary Americans like Carlos Hathcock often preferred to operate alone—but modern doctrine specifies two-man teams. In places like Beirut and Sarajevo, American snipers have done stellar work, waiting patiently in the rubble and ruins of urban combat, and taking as much time as they need to shoot enemy snipers. Snipers have also been employed in Afghanistan and Iraq, and once again their ability to carefully select a target and drop it without fail has been a great help, especially in fighting in and around civilian populations. Snipers also have a very clear role in the war on terror, in that one of the first things any antiterrorist

The typical two-man team, here a USMC sniper with his spotter to his right. After each shot, the spotter, who will not have any recoil to deal with, can quickly tell the shooter where his rounds are impacting down range. A spotter also makes the job of the sniper less creepy and lonesome, although some of the best snipers prefer to hunt alone.

unit does when it gets to a hostage scene or other problem spot is start working out the ranges and lines of fire in case a single shot, or four or five fast ones, can resolve a situation more quickly and safely than any frontal assault ever could.

Well-trained snipers are now one of the cornerstones of many types of operations, as they can hold up much larger enemy units, freeing up your own forces, and also strike precisely at targets like trucks and jets with mostly explosive results. In fighting tanks, snipers can shoot the tank commander if he is up and out of his hatch, or if everything is buttoned up, he can shoot the antennas off and cloud the view port glass with well-placed shots. If they can't talk to HQ and they can't see anything, a tank is just a static display piece.

The modern sniper tends to keep a low profile during peacetime—for instance, there is no sniper badge other than the standard issue marksmanship medals. But that's back on base; out in the field, they really go undercover, and as such they will remain one of the most specialized forms of warfare, and one that can have a devastating effect on an enemy. Excellent shots who are patient and mature enough to become snipers are one of the best tools in the modern military kit, as well as one of the darkest when they go wrong, as Lee Harvey Oswald and the DC sniper showed. Fortunately such lunatics are a minute portion of the men whom our country has trained. The overwhelming majority of American snipers are men who are entirely dedicated to their art, and they have an enthusiasm and verve that sets them apart from almost everyone else. These are the soldiers we rely on to be able to get in position, often in hostile territory, patiently size up what they are looking at, and then with no hesitation pull the trigger and make "one shot, one kill" at our behest.

CHAPTER 6

Spooks in G2: Military Intelligence

ARTHUR WELLESLEY, 1ST DUKE OF Wellington, famously said that he had spent a great deal of his career wondering what was on the other side of a given hill, and military intelligence hasn't actually shifted a lot since his time. Any thoughtful soul faced with prosecuting military endeavors will quickly have a series of questions, to wit: Where is the enemy? How is he equipped? Based on what he has done in the past, what might he be likely to do today/tonight/tomorrow/when we least expect it? It would be nice to think that by now all of this is right down to a well-understood science, and that by simple application of little gray cells the correct answer could be arrived at, communicated where it needs to go, and acted upon in a timely fashion. The reality is far removed from such childish notions, and the most we can say is that American military intelligence is among the best in the world—in other words, vague, contradictory, confusing, spotty, misleading and in the last analysis usually not the decisive factor in warfare.

But it makes a great dream! Why, with good enough intelligence you could do as you pleased, shadow boxing around the tentacles of an enemy and directing his blows against empty air, while you plunge a dagger in his back while he's celebrating his bold strokes of tactical genius. And there are some cases where something close to that happened, such as the numerous Allied triumphs in World War II. However, it seems as if intelligence is too closely linked to human emotions to break free of the fallability and quirky nature of humans, and that the same litany of mistakes is repeated throughout military history with minor variations. All too often the right question isn't asked, or the answer to the right question doesn't get where it needs to go, or the analysis isn't believed, or the enemy does something seemingly "unthinkable." Why this should come as a surprise is just one indication of how poorly most people understand intelligence.

Despite various economic and business applications of spooks following the Cold War, it could be argued that all intelligence worth the name is military in nature. Dance crazes and food fads don't decide history—tanks and jets most certainly do. Ah, but hold on a moment. Knowing details of an enemy can be a crucial advantage in warfare, and that may include what dances they enjoy and how they eat. Because driving those tanks and jets are people who are the product of their own culture, and if they're fatigued by dancing all night and laboring under the weight of a bad empanada, there may be an advantage to be accrued from knowing those facts. You have to give the right weight to everything you find out about an enemy, while also checking for your own personal bias in the analysis. For instance, the cartoon Japanese of propaganda before World War II were bucktoothed and wearing Coke-bottle glasses, and it was widely believed that they couldn't fly airplanes or shoot as well as clear-eyed American boys. The sad truth was that they could fly very well, and fight with a savagery all but unheard of before various Pacific islands had to be retaken inch by inch with little quarter asked or given.

But we're getting ahead of ourselves. It's always best to start with Homer, and consider the fact that Cassandra's great gift was to be able to foretell the future, and to not be believed. Many in the CIA (Central Intelligence Agency) and DIA (Defense Intelligence Agency) would claim this is still the problem. So we have the unhappy picture of Cassandra making dire noises about not taking the big horse inside, while the Trojans are busy putting another line on the thing and picturing where it will best go to brighten up the palace. Or perhaps the legendary trifecta of oracular consultation in Classical times is a better foundation for understanding military intelligence? First we have Croesus standing on the banks of the River Halys, asking the Delphic oracle if he should go ahead and attack the Persians. When the reply came back that if he crossed the river a mighty empire would fall, we may all hope that we would have seen the two-edged nature of that answer—it was his own empire that fell when he crossed.

Then the same Delphic oracle advised the Athenians to trust in their wooden walls as the Persians came rampaging through. But did that mean the walls of the city, or the sides of their great ships? Popular opinion was split, but as it turned out the ships were indeed the right answer, which was cold comfort when the Persians sacked and burned the Acropolis.

And finally we have the Roman admiral who consulted his sacred chickens (I swear I'm not making this up) as to

The ruins of the Temple of Apollo at Delphi in Greece, considered the very center of the ancient world by the Greeks. This isn't where the Oracle hung out—that's in a nearby cave. But you would present your question here, and wait for the priests to bring you the answer, which was often a puzzle cloaked in a riddle wrapped in an enigma ... you'd do better to flip a coin—as with much of modern intelligence work.

whether or not he should attack the Carthaginians. If they ate the sacred wheat, it was a "GO!" and if they ignored it, he should just sail away and wait for another day—or until the sacred chickens were hungry. The sacred chickens evidently wanted nothing to do with the sacred wheat, so the admiral had them thrown overboard, saying "If they will not eat, let them drink." He got creamed.

It could be argued that modern-day spy satellites and communication intercepts have more to do with sacred chickens than they do with some sort of objective under-standing of an enemy's intentions. In each of these four illustrations, the problem was not with the intelligence, but with what use was made of it. Well, perhaps there were a few problems with the intelligence, but it does point out the fact that it's not what you know, but what you do with that knowledge.

Both Sun Tzu and Machiavelli strongly recommended having spies precede any offensive action, and the European nations were gifted at employing all manner of sneakers and peekers, such as the legendary Casanova. In some ages a gentleman could just travel about and keep his eyes and ears open, and then report back, and unless he ran across a particularly vigilant counterintelligence force, the odds were good that most of what needed to be known was out in plain view, such as ships preparing to weigh anchor, or wagons being gathered for a campaign.

The Americans came to military intelligence work with a few hard lessons, such as Braddock's defeat in the French and Indian War. In that case they simply walked into a trap that scouts could have averted; a lesson not lost on one of the survivors, young George Washington. There was also Wolfe's conquest of Quebec, using local knowledge to find and exploit a footpath up to the Plains of Abraham. In both cases the need for a thorough and mature understanding of landscape and tactics made for a staggering defeat and a daring victory, respectively. By the time of the American Revolution, Washington had quite a tidy little unit set up in Manhattan that could get reports out to Long Island, across the Sound to Connecticut, and back to his headquarters in an almost reasonable time. But there is always a price to be paid for sneaking around. When Nathan Hale was hung

The cost of espionage is well-illustrated here by Major Andre, late of His Majesty's army, shown strung up after being caught with compromising maps and letters pertaining to the betrayal of Benedict Arnold during the American Revolution. Just as with Nathan Hale, he came to an end because of poor tradecraft, not a lack of bravery. Such an image of a British officer hanging was designed to provoke outrage, as it was an ignoble death, felt to be only fit for the thousands of poor Irish the British had hung over the years, or those American dogs.

just outside The Yale Club on 44th Street in New York, he became a poster boy for poorly trained and insufficiently discreet operatives who had the nerve and enthusiasm, but not the tradecraft to pursue their calling. On the other side, when Major John Andre was caught by a routine patrol with maps of West Point and incriminating letters in his boot, one of the great traitors in history was forced to wrap up his machinations and flee to England. As to whether any of these operations affected what was happening on the field of battle, the answer seems to be not really.

Napoleon was renowned for his scouts, and was able to turn an entire army on a dime to meet a surprise attack, and yet we have him plunging into Russia in the belief that his

A rare picture of Allan Pinkerton, the head of the Union intelligence service in the Civil War. He was even given a false name in this wet collodion on glass negative, that of "E. J. Allen." Spy chiefs most often do not sit for portraits, and especially not in wartime. This 1862 shot is an oddity. Pinkerton was always suitably mysterious, but couldn't provide good maps of Virginia for another year.

troops could live off the land (they couldn't), while his understanding of the Russian mind led him to believe that if he captured the holy city of Moscow, the czar would sue for peace (he didn't). By the time the mayor of Moscow set fire to the holy city, even Napoleon's staff was wondering what had happened to the great man's legendary instincts. Just another of the eternal lessons of military history: wanting something to be true does not make it so.

The American Civil War featured a great deal of spying, but once again it was like a series of pinpricks rather than any lightning bolt that fell from the heavens and crushed the other team. Confederate spies did manage to start a series of fires in New York City hotels, and Allan Pinkerton

125

certainly expended a great deal of time and money recruiting and running spies and scouts, but he couldn't protect the president on a night out at the theater, and he couldn't provide good maps of Virginia until at least 1863. Anyone who has been bamboozled by a bad map will have some sympathy for the Union commanders who plunged into a series of dusty roads with an entire column behind them, only to conclude angrily that the map didn't reflect what they were seeing in front of them.

Good maps are an absolutely essential requirement of any travel, and their importance is magnified if there are other people likely to be shooting at you as you go on your way. The British had mapped their island by the end of the 1700s, and those are still some of the best maps you'll ever run across; the Ordnance Survey maps have every stone wall, tree line, small stream, and hut marked authoritatively. Some of the Prussian and French maps rivaled the Ordnance Survey, but as had been said, not only do most military actions happen at night in the rain while attacking uphill, but most often the area involved is where the corners of four maps meet. The British also managed to map much of their empire, such as running a survey team along the entire border of Canada with the United States, and unraveling the mysteries of India and Nepal.

World War I, especially at the start, featured all the wishful thinking and misconceptions anybody could want. First, it was that no nation would go to war just because of a little assassination in the Balkans; then it was that the war would be over by Christmas. By 1916 the feeling in the trenches was that the war would go on forever, and that even if they could get home on leave and procreate, their children and grandchildren would be fighting the same war many years

126

Mata Hari in all her glory. She wasn't a very good spy, but she was intrusive enough to be shot, and to pass into legend as a spy queen. Most successful spies don't do exotic dances as a cover, but the legend has proved irresistible. The French counter-intelligence service wasn't fooled for very long.

hence. Military intelligence consisted of any means of finding out more about who was on the other side of No Man's Land, and what they might be doing. This took the form of aerial reconnaissance with the new airplane, observation balloons (which had first been used in the Civil War, and later in the Franco-Prussian War of 1870), as well as frightening night raids. The hope was that you could slink out through the barbed wire, face blackened with soot, and use a cosh on a lone enemy soldier so that he could be transported back to your lines and grilled about his unit and their orders. Some legendary characters made a name for themselves by their proficiency at this crude intelligence gathering, such as the young Erwin Rommel, British poet Sigfried Sassoon, and American poet Joyce Kilmer.

There was also a great deal of behind the lines activities,

127

in places like Paris (think "Mata Hari"), and the first comint (communications intelligence) of much importance when the British passed the so-called Zimmerman telegram along to the Americans. It simply said that the Germans hoped Mexico would attack the southern U.S. border, and that they could have all of Texas and California back if they did. Combined with the sinking of the *Lusitania*, it wasn't long before the standoffish Americans were fielding the AEF and providing fresh blood for a tired conflict.

From about 1900 on, there was a well-understood dance that military intelligence officers engaged in, partly the "Great Game" (which was the UK against the Russians for many years throughout Asia and the Middle East), and partly cocktail party espionage. It was accepted that the military officer at any embassy was there to find out all he could about whatever country he was posted to, and that if he got too frisky, he would be deported (instead of shot), as would perhaps one of his officers at the embassy.

And then you had the amateurs. British author Erskine Childers came out with a great potboiler called *The Riddle of the Sands* concerning a German invasion of England, and the crackpot LeQueux built an entire career around legions of German spies that only he could find, all of them just awaiting "Der Tag" ("The Day") when they would cast off their covers as waiters and language instructors and attack bonny England from within. The British authorities tried to brush these nuts off, but by then the public's imagination was inflamed, not helped by the success of John Buchan's *The Thirty-Nine Steps*, and suddenly everybody was an expert at derring-do and spy work—or so they thought. The reality, then as now, is that the vast majority of intelligence work is done by quiet professional men and women who read a great deal and attempt to put what they know into actionable intelligence, meaning it seems as if X will happen, and we might want to consider doing Y to thwart X.

In the United States, the Office of Naval Intelligence was opened in 1882, because it was mostly a naval world that the new world power America would have to be dealing with. Who had dreadnoughts, how they were being used, and where the coaling stations were located was vital information. Army intelligence was mostly done at dinner parties and embassy functions, and there wasn't any air intelligence just yet—simply the knowledge (brushed off at the highest levels) that airplanes could sink battleships. Consider the fact that by December of 1941 a warning had been out for ten days that the Japanese fleet was up to something, and that our codebreakers were reading most of the high-level stuff. It's too easy to give in to conspiracy thinking, and Roosevelt had obviously been helping Britain against the Germans. But it now appears that despite warnings coming in from every direction, it just could not be understood that the Japanese would seriously consider attacking Pearl Harbor on a Sunday morning.

But for a really sad case of military intelligence mishaps, it's hard to beat the Sovieet response to Operation Barbarossa. Keep in mind that Stalin had executed 75 percent of his officer corps in the late 1930s (believing them to pose the greatest danger to his dictatorship), and the fact that reports started to roll in during the spring of 1941 that seemingly every dang German soldier in the world was poised at the Polish border, and that they were looking east with bad intent. At that time the various Soviet intelligence agencies (NKVD, GRU, etc.) were among the best in the world—and yet they could not get their leader to face the

Part of Operation Fortitude, which was the successful Allied effort to make the Nazis think the real D-Day invasion was coming across the Channel via the most direct route, into the Pas de Calais. To support this notion, there was a dynamic leader (General George S. Patton) of the fake army, a great deal of fake radio traffic, and these Bigbobs, which were canvas stretched over frames and floating on a series of 45-gallon oil drums, and looking remarkably like a Landing Craft Tank Mark II.

fact that his treaty-buddy Hitler might not be on the level. Talk about the sorrows of Cassandra! Twenty million Russian casualties later, the magnitude of this miscalculation is breathtaking in its arrogance and ignorance, in about equal parts.

The United States had by then adopted the staff system that pertains to this day, in that the G-2 of any staff consisted of the intelligence guys. Aerial photo reconnaissance was in its heyday, but subject as always to interpretation—such as when the V2 rockets were thought to be merely scaffolding on their pads at Peenemunde. But World War II also had some of the finest deception plans ever foisted on an eager enemy, and the Abwehr of Admiral Canaris seemed almost suspiciously keen to believe whatever secondhand news came their way. Thus we have German agents in England turned around and sending false reports back, and the clever operation of "The Man Who Never Was" in which an anonymous corpse was dressed up as a Royal Marine officer named Martin, and dropped by submarine off the Spanish coast. Among his papers was clear evidence that the next Allied objective would be Greece—which was entirely not true. Franco's intelligence minions and their Nazi friends took the bait hook, line, and sinker.

For the Normandy landings a deception campaign on an unprecedented scale was launched. This saw the bellicose General George S. Patton placed in charge of a fictitious army that threatened the Pas de Calais—which was not where the landings were going to take place. But so well did this operation use blow-up tanks (to fool German planes) and fake radio traffic, and so great was Patton's reputation as the "go to" guy, that many German divisions were sucked away from Normandy, and even after the D-Day landings began, many German generals thought they were a diversion. By then we were well down the rabbit hole of modern military intelligence: "They think that we think that they think that we think ..." This maddening mantra still has great currency. And it could work both ways, and always can. When the winter storm of Christmas 1944 grounded most Allied planes, the Germans were able to attack quite well at the Battle of the Bulge, although they couldn't keep the campaign going for long once the skies cleared.

A fascinating lawyer from Buffalo named "Wild Bill" Donovan had used his adventurous spirit (he had won the

Medal of Honor in the trenches of France in World War I) and social connections to start the OSS with Roosevelt's blessing as war loomed. The Office of Strategic Services was the forerunner of the CIA, and what Donovan was looking for in his operatives was "an Ivy League PhD who could win a bar fight." The OSS operated around the world and behind the lines, and caused no end of trouble—some to their own side. One operation was the burglary of an embassy in Portugal. Unfortunately, nobody had told the OSS that we had already broken the codes from that embassy, and that due to their "black bag job," all those coded messages we had been reading would now be changed to a code we could not read. But Roosevelt was a tricky and complex man, and he enjoyed pitting all his assets against one another, and then figuring it out for himself. He was a great fan of murder mysteries, and an avid reader of the *New York Times*, and as such he reckoned he was more than able to do his own intelligence analysis. This is a fatal mistake in any leader. Churchill had the same problem, in that he often demanded not the analysis of the people he was paying to analyze, but the original intercepted document. The British, with the help of the Poles and French, had of course broken the Enigma machine codes, and this gave them an unprecedented advantage in fighting the Germans. And why didn't the Germans change their codes, or suspect that their machine could be understood by a clever enemy? Well, it was the finest bit of German engineering that had ever come down the pike, and so it couldn't be cracked ... right? Wrong.

Meanwhile the FBI was feeling threatened by the OSS, and tried to get into the counterintelligence racket on their own in South America and elsewhere. But when a spy

Called "The Last American Hero" by one biographer, William J. "Wild Bill" Donovan was an American original. An Irishman from Buffalo, he nevertheless became a valued member of the Columbia football team (where he picked up the "Wild Bill" moniker), a Medal of Honor winner as the colonel of the Rainbow Division in World War I, the founder of a "white shoe" law firm, and a member of the exclusive Down Town Association in Manhattan—and the founder of the OSS, the forerunner of the modern CIA. He had many detractors as well as admirers, but his biggest fan was FDR, and that was good enough to enable he and his organization to rampage around the world throughout World War II. It was said of him: "Donovan has one hundred astounding ideas a day, and only two of them are good; but those two good ones are corkers." This picture suggests some of the strength and charisma of the man.

Just before the elections in 1968 at the height of the Vietnam War, this group in the Oval Office includes (from left to right around the circle) Sec. of Defense Clark Clifford, Sec. of State Dean Rusk, Jerri Rudolph, Pres. Lyndon Johnson, Asst. Press Secretary Tom Johnson, Walt Rostow, Gen. Earle Wheeler, and DCI and CIA Director Richard Helms, aka "The Man Who Kept the Secrets." Helms had cleverly been standing to one side when the Bay of Pigs went south, and then ascended to DCI status in time to shred a mountain of documents as tall as the Washington Monument pertaining to strange and illegal CIA machinations. He also tried to get the intelligence reports from Vietnam to sound like we were winning, but his own analysts revolted at this canard. Special Bonus: Is there a Soviet supermole named "Sascha" in this picture?

named Dusko Popov tried to warn J. Edgar Hoover about Pearl Harbor, Hoover didn't like the cut of his jib and dismissed the information. What are we to make of so many leaders brushing off good intelligence like it was a pestering bellhop? Hubris and pride make for fuzzy thinking.

After the war, it became apparent that the next enemy would be the Soviet Union, so the United States struck a deal with a Nazi named Gehlen, who had run the Soviet section of German military intelligence. This provided us with a great deal of information about the other side, and only a few spoilsports kicked up a fuss about working with Nazis. The CIA was created in 1947, and started off first by missing the North Korean attack that started the Korean War, and then the Chinese intervention. In the meantime, the atomic bomb secrets had been stolen and gone abroad. It seemed as if somebody didn't understand this business too well.

In a series of pinprick attacks, U.S. military intelligence worked with the CIA to try to destabilize the Soviets wherever it could be accomplished, and as a result we wound up backing a lot of right-wing dictatorships just because they weren't communist, and laid the seeds for the intelligence failures of today. Probably the low points of military intelligence were the Vietnam War, which was misreported at every step right up until we had to leave, and the systemic over-reporting of Soviet capabilities. This made defense manufacturers happy, and wasted a great deal of money over the years. The Soviets were indeed cunning and dangerous, but they couldn't match the monetary output of the United States any better than the Germans could. As late as 1985 they were still using horse-drawn wagons to move half their army, and while that's good up to a point, it's hardly the mark of a truly mighty enemy.

With the rise of technology, especially the satellite and computer, an entirely new realm of misunderstanding became available to G-2 wonks everywhere. Now there was so much information it was like trying to drink out of a firehose, and finding the silver bullet among the shaken trees was harder than ever. You could also simply refuse to believe what the intelligence was telling you, or not act upon it.

135

The modern face of U.S. intelligence is a $40-billion monster that vacuums up an unbelievable amount of stuff, and then tries to get it understood and sent back out to the people who need to understand it. This task is mighty simple in outline, and fantastically complicated in practice. You start collecting data: "Do the Chinese have a new attack helicopter?" Then you simply troll though a trough of data the size of the Pacific, including fuzzy photos on the Internet and satellite shots from overhead, see what your embedded spies have to say, look at what they've done in the past, and try to boil all that down into a definitive document. But the hidden message behind most of these reports is "maybe."

But it doesn't pay to get too cynical about intelligence. Sometimes the right answer is produced, and it can be remarkably helpful to have the information ahead of time. Keep in mind that "information" is not "intelligence." Intelligence has been chewed over and connected in context, and you can do something with it. Two recent examples are almost too painful to discuss, and yet they are at the root of the two most recent military operations that the United States has embarked upon: the surprise attack on September 11, 2001, and the threat of weapons of mass destruction in Iraq. In the first case, we had about all the warning anybody is likely to get in this world, such as the fact that the World Trade Center had already been a target, there was a thwarted 1995 mass hijacking of airliners, Osama bin Laden had said clearly he wished to strike us at home, known al Qaeda operatives were slipping into the United States and learning to fly, etc. And yet we didn't know where, when, and how exactly. In the case of WMDs, it sure seemed that if anyone had such things or was loony enough to use them, it was Sadaam Hussein. But taking the word of treacherous weasels like Mr. Chelabi, and then trying to link Hussein to bin Laden, showed the opposite problem from 9/11, in the spirit of "Don't just stand there—DO something!" But it isn't the best idea to make political fodder of all this—fresh intelligence failures await the righteous and hubristic. You also have to put your mind back into the pre-9/11 world mindset—and then think what you would do in the wake of such an event.

Fortunately, at the lower levels, you can make your very own mistakes with whatever filters down to you through the system. Despite this, many excellent S2 (or G2) officers and enlisted men do a great job of putting together all the pieces, and giving to their commanders the best intelligence available when it is needed. This can include everything from the weather to the terrain, and such finicky points as when the sun will vanish, and if there is a moon on a given night. In some kinds of warfare this is easier than others. For instance, one of the hardest situations for an intelligence officer is fighting a guerilla war among a hostile population, with a religion and a culture you don't understand, and where the enemy can strike and fade away. Gathering information may not be a problem, but getting good intelligence out of that information can be next to impossible. If any of these fighters would form up into companies and battalions, we could just shell them into oblivion. Lacking that, they have to work with the civilian population and try their hardest to segregate the guerillas from the people, all the while trying to figure out what their exit strategy would be that doesn't leave a worse situation than the one they walked into.

Today's intelligence officers and NCOs are expected, despite all difficulties, to provide concise and clear reports

A modern group of intelligence leaders in 2002, from left to right: FBI Director Robert Mueller III, CIA Director George Tenet, Attorney General John Ashcroft, and Homeland Security Director Tom Ridge. Princetonian Mueller is known as "Bobby Three Sticks" among the rank and file, who still don't like to play nice with the CIA; Tenet resigned in 2004 as a sacrificial scapegoat to such intelligence failures as 9/11 and missing WMDs; Ashcroft is viewed by some historians as a major threat to the freedoms in the Constitution; and Tom Ridge is seen as a decent guy with an impossible job and no clear powers or mandate. When Ashcroft and Mueller had a press conference in June of 2004 to make dire noises about attacks in this election year, they didn't consult Ridge or Tenet, which seemed odd to most observers. When Secretary of Defense Rumsfeld didn't like the stuff he was getting from these guys, he set up his own in-house intel unit. Military intelligence hasn't gotten any easier over the years—back to Delphi!

on a daily basis that will enable commanders in the field to take the right action to win—and that means passing the right intelligence at just the right time, and then laying out the options that can be used to accomplish their aims. There are still men who go forward to use the "Mark One Eyeball" to report back what they have seen on the ground, and we will always have as much sigint (signals intelligence), comint (communications intelligence) and elint (electronic intelligence) as they can stand to wade through, but it may be that the Rangers and SEALs and Delta troopers will give the most current and accurate picture of how things stand, and in that we have changed very little from Alfred the Great.

But a famous military historian has also said in a recent book that warfare is not an intellectual activity—managing to spook every other military historian who read his words. He contends that it is by force alone that things are decided on the battlefield, and that the evidence points to intelligence as being just a lot of tail chasing. Don't tell this to the DIA, NSA, NRO, or any of the service intelligence staffs, though. It seems that from all we know, intelligence can be misunderstood, ignored, misinterpreted, cherry-picked (where you just take the parts that back up your conclusion and leave the inconvenient facts to one side), spun, and flat out done wrong and arrive at the wrong conclusion—but that you're surely sunk without it. There are many more cases of countries that missed the opening bell—Pearl Harbor, Korea, Barbarrossa, the Falklands—than there are of those that used intelligence in just the right way to either take just the right action or avoid some dreadful pitfall, but that doesn't mean we cannot or should not keep trying. Interestingly, it doesn't seem as if high tech will cut it in the realm, either. It takes a very smart and mature person to put all the pieces together and get the right answer, and they don't grow on trees. The next intelligence surprises could be a coup in Pakistan or Saudi Arabia, or offensive actions by the North Koreans or the Chinese against Taiwan. But you can bet your bottom dollar that in light of recent events, U.S. military intelligence is working night and day to not have events overtake them again.

CHAPTER 7

Alone on the Battlefield: Escape and Evasion

OF THE MANY undesirable experiences that warfare offers to the participant, from death to maiming wounds, as well as "combat stress" (today's shell shock) and the inability to ever explain the horror of the whole thing when you get back home, perhaps none is more unsettling than being cut off from your fellow soldiers and having to make your way to safety alone. And add to that the specter of being captured, and hauled off to some godforsaken hellhole of a prison. The U.S. military has spent a lot of time thinking about these occurrences and trying to ensure that in the event of such a happening, their soldiers and sailors and airmen and marines will have a tool kit up their sleeve to try to reach as good an outcome as can be managed. And interestingly, the main piece of gear needed is a well-tuned mind. Of course, it wouldn't hurt to have a map, compass, radio, sleeping bag, binoculars, sunglasses, and a good pistol, assault rifle, or submachine gun, but often it is not possible to plan such an outing with the same foresight as a family jaunt to the Grand Canyon or Yellowstone. For that reason the realm of SERE (survival, evasion, resistance, and escape) begins with an attitude, and builds from the inside out.

In earlier forms of warfare, prisoners were either slain summarily on the field, or else dragged back home as slaves, the Romans being the best-known proponents of this method of avoiding doing one's own dishes. It was fairly well understood what would happen to the losers in any kind of violent dust up, and soldiers harbored few illusions about the possible outcomes of failure. Sometimes this "do or die" mentality could be an aid to desperate fighting. We have the case of the conquistador who burned his ships upon arrival in the New World: "There! Let's hear no more whining about how you wish you could get back to Spain! This is our only world now!" There was also the extraordinary story of Cabeza de Vaca, who got separated from his men in Florida and somehow got to Mexico, sometimes as a prisoner or slave, and sometimes as a holy man among the native peoples. He didn't look so good when he finally linked up with his team many hundreds of miles and years later—but he made it. Why didn't he give up, as many of us probably would have? For reasons known best to themselves, for every case of a person dying on the spot when faced with a survival situation, there are men like Hugh Glass, the fur trapper and mountain man who, after being mauled by a grizzly bear and abandoned by his comrades (one of whom was a young Jim Bridger, later to become a famed mountain man and scout himself) because of the "obviously" fatal nature of his wounds, managed to first crawl to water, and then to crawl more than a hundred miles to civilization. There's no reliable record of what exactly he said to the men who had forsaken him when they met up years later, but mountain men were never noted for the delicacy of their vocabularies, although they did aspire to a certain laconic understatement. Perhaps a simple "Howdy" sufficed.

But throughout history, if you weren't killed on the battlefield, chances were you would be dragged off to pull an oar as a galley slave, as happened to the Spanish author Cervantes, or if you were of sufficient social standing you might have some value as a hostage, as happened to Richard the Lionheart on his way home from the Crusades. But if you weren't a king, you could expect the worst sort of treatment, bad food, hard work, illness, torture if they even cared enough to torture you, and eventual death in the meanest of conditions. Lord Byron's poem "Sonnet on Chillon," which begins: "Eternal Spirit of the chainless Mind! / Brightest in dungeons, Liberty! thou art, / For there thy habitation is the heart," wonderfully captures the soul-crushing aspect of such lone confinement, and the daily struggle to overcome a meaningless and constricted life, as well as the moments of mental triumph that could come from such small things as a ray of sunlight or a passing bird. It's all about attitude.

During the American Revolution there were the dreaded prison ships, in both England and British-occupied New York harbor, where men were kept in the vilest of conditions aboard the rotting hulks of unusable sailing ships. The addition of huge rats did nothing for the overall tenor of the

The dire scene at the dreaded Andersonville Prison in Georgia, where malignant neglect and active starvation combined to kill many prisoners before their time. Poor clothing and overcrowding helped the misery index to soar, and infectious disease ran rampant through these poor men. Conditions at prisons in the North were no better, but Andersonville is a name that will always elicit a shudder from anyone who knows its story.

experience. The horrific conditions encountered at such legendary Civil War prisons as Andersonville have been well documented, although there were some cases where prisoners were simply disarmed and sent home, or exchanged for the enemy's prisoners. Interestingly the end of the war featured one of the noble acts of the conflict, when General Ulysses S. Grant returned General Robert E. Lee's sword to him at Appomattox. But the years following that conflict were not marked by overmuch charity and forgiveness on either side, and the depredations of the "carpetbaggers" were a sore spot for generations of Southerners.

One of the great classics of literature, Crane's *The Red Badge of Courage* gives us some insight into the mind of a young man who, after being overwhelmed by his first taste of combat and wandering around the battlefield, comes in time to rejoin his unit and take a meaningful part in the next assault. There is no way of knowing at this great remove from the Civil War how many men deserted, or simply left the field and joined back up later. We do know that thousands and thousands were captured and died in the meanest of conditions, weakened by lack of food and medical care to the point where they simply couldn't go on living. This terrible aspect of warfare hasn't changed a bit, despite some attempts to make things a little better for prisoners, notably by the Red Cross. In both world wars the record was spotty, from executions on the battlefield (by all sides) to prison camps that ranged from the almost decent to the absolutely horrific. German prison camps were no better than they had to be, although it seems they were quite a step up from the ones the Japanese ran. These featured every sort of brutality and death, as well as barbaric medical exams. And episodes like the Bataan Death March gave new insight into cruelty and savage mistreatment.

One heartening contrast to this sorry, ongoing story is the German prisoners who were interned in rural Maine, some of whom liked it so well and were so decently treated by the locals that they moved there after World War II and settled down. This stands out as a pretty rare case. In Kenya there were two Italians in a British camp who escaped so they

American prisoners using improvised litters are seen here trying to save sick and exhausted men from the brutality of their Japanese captors during the infamous Bataan Death March in May of 1942. If Pearl Harbor wasn't enough, once word got out about this demonic march, American soldiers were good and mad by the time they hit the beaches in the Pacific.

could climb Mount Kenya, which they had been staring at for months. The British themselves made rather a parlor game of escape, such as the famous use of a vaulting horse to cover a tunnel, and the phenomenal prisoners of Colditz Castle, who somehow managed to find a way to freedom, including the building of a glider in the unused attic. It seems that there are some men who, if you stick them in a hole, will not lay down but will just hitch up their pants and go to work to try to find a way out. While there may be more fiction than fact to the bestseller *Papillion*, nevertheless it captures this spirit well, and the fact that anyone got off Devil's Island is amazing enough in itself. The same could be said for the missing prisoners who seem to have gotten away from Sing Sing, as their bodies and raft were never found. Anyone familiar with the cold water and powerful

146

currents of San Francisco harbor would think long and hard before launching off in a small unseaworthy craft to try to brave those dark waters.

The Korean War brought an entirely new and unwelcome aspect to POW issues, in that the North Koreans and Chinese not only attempted to break their prisoners by beatings, but also engaged in extensive "brainwashing" experiments, with less than successful results, other than to make the experience even more miserable than it had previously been. They also seem to have kept some prisoners for decades. By the time of Vietnam there were no illusions about what captivity among the communists might mean for Americans, and for the first time extensive training was given to pilots and others who might find themselves down in the jungle with no friends nearby. WWII pilots had been given such things as silk maps sewn into their flight jackets, and tiny compasses, as well as some idea about who to contact to start the process of trying to get back to England (usually through Spain), but in Vietnam for the first time a real science was made out of Combat Search & Rescue (CSAR) as well as general survival issues. This seemed like a wise move in a country of impenetrable undergrowth and such fauna as the 18-foot-long cobra and the ever-irascible tiger—to say nothing of the Viet Cong and NVA troops who always worked extra hard to get an American prisoner. And if the men were captured, places like the Hanoi Hilton were legendary for their brutality, as Senator John McCain can attest, as well as for the undaunted courage that men like him showed in the most appalling conditions. The fact that his service has been attacked by men who were not there is simply beyond comprehension. Politics may be the only thing more brutal and disheartening than warfare.

A propaganda shot of an American pilot being given first aid by a North Vietnamese captor. Many pilots were simply shot out of hand, or else tortured and displayed in various small villages on their way to the Hanoi Hilton and other hellhole prisons. Almost 1,000 men are still missing in action from that sad war, including pilots, SOG troopers like Jerry "Mad Dog" Shriver, and CIA operatives from Air America.

The early CSAR was an ad hoc system to start with, in that when a plane went down the balloon went up, and every friendly unit for about one hundred miles started thinking how they could help with the rescue. The legendary American helicopter pilots of the Vietnam War pulled off some astounding rescues, often under heavy fire, and sometimes when quite elaborate traps had been set for them. There were all sorts of pitfalls for the early days of such an inherently dangerous operation, such as the enemy using our radios to suck us in, or trying to use one of their men in one of our flight suits to attract attention. Fortunately, Americans are nothing if not clever, and the defense against such tricks could take many forms. One man's date of birth was used as an indicator that he should move in that direction (the numbers being understood to mean compass bearings by the man on the ground); another famous rescue hinged on the fact that both men on the radio had played the same golf courses and remembered their layouts, making for a completely incomprehensible radio transmission that nonetheless managed to steer the man on the ground to the rescue chopper. Pilots carried marking smoke of various colors, and it would take a very literate and culturally adept enemy to understand that the request to "pop goofy grape" was a reference to a crystal drink popular in the United States, and that purple was the appropriate smoke canister to pull the ring on to mark a downed pilot's position.

This cleverness comes up a lot in POW and survival stories, such as the propaganda film shot in a North Vietnamese prison of an American pilot that showed him spouting a lot of communist nonsense while meantime blinking his eyes in the Morse code that spelled out "torture"—kudos to the intelligence analyst who looked at that and remembered his dashes and dots. Unfortunately, the massive rescue operation that descended on Son Tay prison camp west of Hanoi came up empty handed, because the prisoners had been moved due to the potential flooding of a local river. The Son Tay rescue failed because timely intelligence wasn't passed down the line.

In 1980 the United States launched a massive operation to try to release the Americans held hostage in Iran, and that failed even more spectacularly due to the effort being compromised by accidents at the staging area at Desert One in Iran. Due to this failure the presidency of the United States changed hands, but another result was that the Special Forces community was drawn together for the first time in

Air Force Captain Scott F. O'Grady raises his arms in triumph after six days on the ground in Bosnia following his shoot down, and a daring rescue that swooped in and scooped him up in June of 1995. Would that all shot-down pilots could feel this same exhilaration.

Special Operations Command, and the American method of pulling off such impossible missions was fine-tuned to a faretheewell by endless thought, training, and practice. By the time Scott O'Grady went down in the 1990s while flying above the former Yugoslavia, a well-oiled machine sprang into action and coordinated a massive array of assets to eventually extract him despite the best efforts of the Serbs to nail his butt to the wall.

Today there are two clear parts to this exercise: there is the person on the ground, who needs to do his/her best to keep their head in the game and keep pushing, and then there are the CSAR assets, from Pararescue Jumpers (PJs) to P3 Orion and AWACs overhead, and all of these have the same end in mind. Get that person out of there and back under friendly control. Think of what the average downed pilot is faced with. He/she is now a lone wolf being hunted on the ground. The mess hall back at the airfield or the galley aboard the aircraft carrier is no more than a distant dream. Pilots tend to get the most training for this, as it is they who are most often to be found behind the lines, no longer wearing their multimillion-dollar aircraft; and in today's world they cannot count on any friendly locals to take them in and feed them into a pipeline that leads back to home, as in World War II. It may well be that every part of the operation involves hostile people who would like nothing better than the PR coup of an American to display on Al Jazeera.

But despite all the dire considerations that may creep into your thinking, the basics go right back to Lord Byron and Hugh Glass: if you think you can make it, maybe you can; if you don't think you can make it, for sure you will not. So to start a downed pilot needs to get clear of the wreckage if he's crash landed, or hide his parachute if he's "hit the silk" to escape a jet that started behaving like a concrete block. But wait a minute! Might he need that parachute? Parachutes make dandy shelters, and can be used for signaling to friendly aircraft, and he could even make a little dew catcher out of it if he suspends it between four points and puts a rock on the middle and a can underneath. Because, after all, he has got to take care of himself, and

151

water is going to be something he needs above all else, including food. And then he needs to take a moment to sit down and carefully consider the lay of the land, just how things are, and what might most profitably happen next. The options do not include panic or despair—both are a waste of time and energy. Because how he feels about things is going to materially affect the outcome, and there is absolutely no debate on this point. If he gives in to bad thoughts, he'll just tire out and run around in circles wasting time. What he needs instead is a plan—and the right training.

Hopefully he watched his maps during the time when he was flying, and has some idea of where the cardinal points are located, and where the friendly team has its lines. In the civilian world you are supposed to stay with your air-

A group of aeromedical students undergoing SERE training set off some rescue flares in Texas. The length of the course varies, but this one is five days of laying low, working with the landscape, thinking and acting like the natives, and eluding captors and hostile locals while awaiting rescue. At that time, such a flare would signal the PJs where they need to get to in order to commence an evac at high speed.

craft/car/boat in case of a problem, as it makes for a large and easy thing to find from the air. But in a combat environment, ditching that big marker as quickly as you can, and get moving is more the order of the day. He may have to hole up for awhile, but he should always be trying to get back somehow under his own steam if his condition will allow. Fortunately, the world is full of markers, in that the sun comes up in the east and goes down in the west, and is at its highest point at local noon, and in the northern hemisphere that is about due south. At night the moon replicates the movements of the sun, and various easy-to-spot constellations such as the Big Dipper, Orion's Belt, Cassiopeia's Chair, and the Southern Cross are blazing bright indicators of how things are laid out. The world is not just a dangerous place full of enemy soldiers and big cobras; it is a finite and understandable system that can lead someone right back to his own front door if he can read the signs correctly. At sea, the presence of shore birds, clouds on the horizon, and seaweed can indicate where there is dry land, and the ancient Polynesians could even read the swells and currents to spot islands. With a little knowledge and practice, it is possible to move over almost any terrain and get where you would like to be with only some good shoes and the will to keep going. Lost your boots? Make new ones. Cardboard can be used for a sole, and cloth can be used to wrap your ankles. Sun too bright? Improvise glacier shades as the ancient Eskimos did by making an eye covering with a small slit to see through. If it's hot, make a hat. If it's cold, try to dress in layers, polypro near the skin, fleece as a barrier layer, and some sort of rain and windproof gear over the top. And if it's dumping rain, don't forget to collect some for drinking.

For hacking around behind enemy lines one needs to conceal oneself from them and yet still be able to attract attention when a Pave Low with U.S. markings shows up, so camouflage is more than appropriate. you need to break up the outline of your body as a sniper would, as well as your distinctive head and face outlines which can be detected at quite long range. When moving, one will want to stay low and follow not the top of a ridge, but just below it so your silhouette doesn't stand out against the sky. It's best not to walk in a river (unless you're being tracked by men and/or dogs), but to follow it carefully from twenty yards back from the bank. Constructing a raft and trying to shoot downstream to safety is a good idea only with a fair amount of caution: anyplace where the river displays a sharp edge ahead, and you can see the tops of trees beyond that, is a place you won't wish to negotiate in a raft or any other craft. You need to listen for the noise of the water as well. If it's too loud to hear yourself think, chances are good that there's some god-awful cataract just ahead.

If you can make some progress toward safety and get away from your plane, pretty soon weariness will set in. Then a spot for sleeping needs to be chosen, either in natural cover such as a cave or among some large trees, or by using your parachute as a shelter, which you may have to disguise with

154

There's always plenty of stuff to eat in most forests and jungles, although it may prove useful to think of something else when you bite into a toad, as this Marine is doing during a jungle survival class at Camp Butler. You always need to think before you start biting things, though—there's some bad stuff out there, and some South American tribes use poison from the back of toads to kill small game with bows or blowguns. This makes dinner a trying event.

branches and leaves. If you have food or can gather a little, you need to debate the wisdom of starting a fire. The good part about a fire is that it is an immediate morale boost. For some reason, probably going back to our cave-dwelling ancestors, nothing says "It's going to be all right" as well as a cheery little blaze. But the smoke could give you away to your pursuers, so you may have to eat and drink whatever you have cold and call it good, perhaps taking refuge in the Russian folk saying "With food comes hope."

Traveling by compass in wilderness areas is not an innate gift. Practice can make you more confident, but even hardened outdoors types get lost now and then, so it's best to just figure that it's part of the deal and keep trying to make good on your intended course. In most parts of the world today it's best to avoid the local populace, unless there is something they have that you can steal without provoking a full-scale posse reaction. And what's in your survival kit may have a tremendous bearing on the nature of your experience. For instance, the humble signaling mirror is a great item that doesn't get damaged when wet and can be used to contact friendly forces many dozens of miles away. It can be tested by aiming at a stake or fellow evader out ahead of you just off the line to where you are trying to signal, and use that to tell when you've got the angle right. Survival manuals also say to try sweeping the horizon a few times a day if it is safe to do so—you'd be amazed at how far away a little bit of reflected sunlight can be seen.

Because the American military operates in so many diverse climates and parts of the world, special tricks will be needed depending on whether the downed pilot is in a desert or on a glacier. In deserts, you need to beware of the great cold that can come at night, whereas when on a glacier, it can be the deadly crevasses that can be covered by an inch of snow and ice that are your nemesis. In either a desert or the Arctic, one also needs to be aware of the inborn tendency of humans to veer to the left if they walk with no visual clues. You can try this in a field sometime with a friend to spot your progress, but it is a horrifying reality; you'll think you're going straight, and instead you're very gradually going around in a circle. Hardly anything crushes morale more than the realization that you have been walking in a circle.

In case of capture, military personnel are only obligated

Every civilian's nightmare is just a day at the pool to these Marines, who are training in the Modular Amphibious Egress Training Simulator (MAET), which is a fuselage section designed to help them find the exit after their aircraft goes down in the water. It's rolling to the right and filling up with water, indicating that a fast plan and exit will work better than a lot of pondering and argument about where the door might be.

to give their name rank and serial number, but this has a history of angering enemy forces. The military survival manual says not to fold any maps to display where you were going, and to not touch your destination with your finger to prevent there being a telltale smudge at that point. According to current doctrine, you are to maintain your discipline and hope in case of capture, and make every effort to escape. Failing that, the ranking person is in charge of American prisoners, and should make every effort to see

that they are treated decently. But you are supposed to never stop trying to escape, and this despite the worsening treatment your attempts will garnish. Interestingly, under international law if you hurt or kill your captors you are liable to whatever sort of court proceedings they think appropriate—seems like a rather one-way deal. But men can escape from anywhere, and failing that they have maintained their honor and discipline despite the worst efforts that the human mind can devise. It will never be easy, but it can and has been done.

An instructor is shown inspecting the framework of a primitive shelter made by students of the French 5th Marine Battalion. It looks pretty tidy, and is ready for a covering made of, say, a parachute, which will reflect heat and keep the wind off the occupants. Working with local materials, and with some knowledge of how primitive peoples stay warm and dry at night, it is possible for the calm and collected man behind the lines to make quite a good shelter in half a day, and then focus on food and water issues.

But let's back up to the pilot still running free in the bush, when a friendly unit spots him. If he can make radio contact, great, but he needs to keep in mind who else may have a radio. Transmissions should be brief and to the point. In the absence of a radio, he'll watch for things like pilots waggling their wings. This is one way they may communicate. The next thing that happens should be the arrival of two helicopters, an Alpha and a Bravo bird, and they will probably come in low and fast. The two are for redundancy and in case one needs to protect the other. Pararescue Jumpers (PJs) may parachute down, in which case the pilot will have a new friend on the ground, and fortunately he will be one of the most highly trained and competent people on the planet. PJs are not only exceptional paramedics trained for all sorts of wounds and injuries, but they also pack a great deal of firepower, and can call in more when and if they need it.

The ride out may be as simple as getting aboard a helicopter (as it was for Scott O'Grady), or the pilot may be hooked into a harness and either hoisted up or snatched off the ground by a fixed wing aircraft (the so-called "McGuire"

The mighty HH-60G Pave Hawk helicopter is seen here deploying Pararescuemen into Lake George on a training mission. The Pave Hawk has all weather capability, and a 200-foot cable that can lift 600 pounds. This is the CSAR champion today, fast, stealthy, and deploying some of the most highly trained and motivated soldiers to ever take the field on flights of mercy. These guys are known for their big medical bags, panoply of weapons, and grand sense of humor.

160

rig), or he may have to hoof it to a better location with his new friend. Either way, he is back in the net, and the entire resources of the U.S. military will move heaven and earth to make sure he gets the care and attention he deserves. This is a great comfort to pilots for obvious reasons. The helicopters will have miniguns mounted everywhere they can get a pintle to fit, and thus can hose down the surrounding area if would-be captors are anywhere in sight.

Because of the importance that we place on the individual, U.S. policy has always been to try very damn hard to recover anyone who finds themselves behind enemy lines. This is as true in Iraq as anywhere else, and while the rescue of Private Jessica Lynch seems to be a case of the PR machine spinning things a little too hard, it was still a pretty good operation in that the hospital was secured by U.S. Army Rangers, and then a smaller assault and rescue team forced their way in and secured the young soldier. In this way some rescues are rather like raids, in that the intention is not to take ground, but instead to use speed and surprise to accomplish daring and fast strikes into enemy territory, and then get the hell out as safely as possible. There is a security team that guards the perimeter, and then the smaller team has the medical people surrounded by shooters and door kickers.

But all of this takes a little practice. Fortunately, the United States is a large and diverse country, and there are numerous facilities to teach all the fine aspects of survival, escape, rescue, evasion, and how to swoop in and snatch people. The SERE school up by Rangeley, Maine, is rather famous among the locals, and it features thousands of acres of the most terrible undergrowth that the Pine Tree State can offer, as well as bogs, cliffs, mountains, rivers, ponds, and

U.S. Navy SEALs use a poncho half as an improvised litter to medevac a hurt comrade to a waiting chopper in this exercise in Hawaii. If somebody cannot or should not walk (such as with a spinal injury) they have to be carried, and four men is about the minimum amount that will get the job done. Civilian mountain rescue teams say that eighteen people is the minimum number for a litter evac: six on the litter, six ahead, and six behind, trading off. You have no idea how heavy people are until you begin carrying their dead weight. But in combat, any help is much appreciated by wounded soldiers.

the dreaded "black fly" (in season). Other fine schools are down in Florida (think "swamp"), and up in Alaska, as well as a few tucked away in classified locations like Point Harvey.

This topic has also excited an endless stream of manuals to help teach the successful survivor, and these range from the Air Force's tidy doorstop (at 620 pages) down to a very handy booklet on "Survival, Evasion and Recovery" that is a multiservice world-beater. And it fits in your pocket easily. It's rather interesting to compare and contrast these two official publications, in that obviously some deletions and editing has been necessary to get a smaller version, but they both start and end with your state of mind. The little one starts with a great little summation: SURVIVAL, standing for "Size up the situation, surroundings, physical condition, equipment. Use all your sense. Remember where you are. Vanquish fear and panic. Improvise and improve. Value living. Act like the natives. Live by your wits." They both go into building a team (if with others) and the importance of planning and leadership, and even cover spiritual and psychological issues. And while they both have more than enough information on plants and knots, navigation and signaling, recovery and evasion, fire starting and water gathering, both manuals come down to the basics at regular intervals throughout their pages: the bottom line is the will to survive, and the drive to keep pushing and make it so. Something tells me John McCain and Hugh Glass would understand.

CHAPTER 8

Build and Blow: Combat Engineers

As ANY HOME handyman knows, working with tools is tricky in and of itself. The chisel that slips, the vice that bites, the hammer that goes astray and produces a stream of curse words—all will be familiar to Mr. Fixit from his week-end debacles. Just consider how subtle and complex can be the nuances of two things we take for granted in the every-day developed world: plumbing and electricity. Getting that arm to come back up and stop the commode from running, and making sure that everything is grounded and up to code, can occupy as much time and thought as you care to throw at them.

Yet there is an entire world of building (and unbuilding) that goes as far beyond this as a 777 compared to a balsa wood glider. When a combat engineer is called on the scene, he/she will have a world of options, most of them less than

164

perfect, and usually the most awful conditions in which to somehow fix (or unfix) a full range of projects. At the most basic level it is said that combat engineers convert "no go" terrain into "go" terrain, and vice versa; that they work for mobility and antimobility as the shifting tactical and strategic situation demands—either fording a river by pontoons and improvised bridges, or else preventing the other side from crossing. Because so much of warfare is and always has been about maneuver and "getting there first with the most," the role of the combat engineer runs along like a rhythm section behind the melody of war, an integral supporting part that is often lost in the shuffle. But nothing gets done without that beat.

There has always been a distinct carryover from civilian engineering into the realm of combat, and this began quite early with such luminaries as Archimedes, who was renowned for his siege machines as much as for his famous screw, or the bath that told him how to measure and weigh awkward items. Siege warfare was a natural for the leader and men who knew how to put things together, and perhaps thereby get other things to fall apart. The legendary Trojan horse probably qualifies as the first anecdotal piece of combat engineering, in that it was a clever way to break a siege. But notice how even in that operation there needed to be a plan and a great deal of supporting activity. They had to have the assault team within the equine red herring, and then the rest of the Greek army making every appearance of packing up to get back on their ships and leave Helen to enjoy her housekeeping in Asia Minor, while actually being prepared to rush back to the gates when the inside team got them open.

Archimedes, perhaps the first combat engineer, is shown here thinking about sieges, as shown by the ships attacking a castle before him, and the siege tower to the right, which could be rolled up to a castle wall and used to tunnel under the foundation or attack the ramparts, while shielding the attackers from arrows and boiling pitch. The protractor in his hand is still in use for navigation, and very handy they are, too.

Many of the engineering triumphs and legends of the ancient world will excite envy from the modern engineer in that manpower was never seemingly a problem. Build two mile-long piers out to the city of Tyre (as Alexander did)? Not a problem! Cross raging rivers and high icy mountains with funky animals (as Hannibal did)? Can do! Dam and redirect a river to drown out the capital of the Sybarites? Consider it done! It's also a theme that many of the great commanders throughout history had a great respect and knowledge of engineering, if they weren't engineers themselves, such as Robert E. Lee. Part of the essential tool kit of any commander is having a realistic sense of the terrain and the features within it that can be used to shoot your men forward, such as a dry riverbed, or provide a safe flank, such as the ocean. But that realism has to be tempered by history: the greatest loss of lives in a single incident among the Green Berets in Vietnam was an assault by Viet Cong sappers that hit a beachfront base from the sea—you have to carefully consider just how safe your "safe flank" really might be.

There is always something risky about water in any connection with military matters. Your entire bellicose endeavor can be stopped by a thundering cataract while your enemy has found a ford five miles upstream, or you can simply drown in it if you are so unwise as to carry heavy things like weapons and armor on your next swimming outing. When the Roman Emperor Maxentius was drowned on his pontoon bridge across the Tiber by the forces of Constantine in 312 AD, he was neither the first nor the last commander to fail during a river crossing. Interestingly, in that battle the engineers had made one section of the bridge so that it could be collapsed in case the enemy wished to use it, and it was that section that threw the emperor into the deadly Tiberian flow. Napoleon's career featured both triumph and tragedy at rivers, be it the bridges of Italy that made his reputation as a leader who could surge to victory from the very front ranks, to the terrible waterways of Russia which, perversely, thawed during a blisteringly cold autumn and winter at all the worst moments in his horrific retreat of 1812. Only by the most extreme efforts on the part of the French engineers were bridges constructed and crossings found for the shabby remnants of a once-great army.

Early American engineers had one good advantage, in that from the start there stretched out in front of them a large continent with no structure more complicated than an Algonquin longhouse and some earthen mounds anywhere from Machias, Maine, to San Diego, California. If there were to be a new country, it would have to be built. And the first thing that was needed was shelter, followed shortly by a palisade fence, which was a series of logs with the tops sharpened set upright in the ground, in hopes that violent locals wouldn't come swarming at you in the middle of a dark night. The palisade was far from perfect, as was shown during the Deerfield raid of 1704, when Native Americans led by French officers used snowbanks to ascend the logs.

Engineering could be said to be the forgotten linchpin of America, although among a certain set the challenges and accomplishments of American engineering still shine like a bright light in human endeavor, from the work of Colonel Knox in getting the cannons from Ticonderoga to Boston, to the modern vehicles and technology that make the United States military machine without equal in the world. Who else would dig a canal from Albany to Buffalo, or push a railroad across the continent, or dam the mighty rivers for power, or provide the world with electric light, telegraphs and telephones (and run cable under the sea to talk to Europe), steamships, locomotives, airplanes, cars, trucks, small arms and artillery, and missiles that can escape the planet's gravitational pull? All of this and more are the legacy of the wonks and nerds of their day, and interestingly they were seen as rather sexy visionaries for their work. There was a time when the man with the slide rule showed up, and mighty things were done, transferred from paper to reality in breathtakingly short time periods, and wondered at by the gaping masses. Just take a glance at the Brooklyn Bridge sometime and imagine the almost insane confidence it took to thrust those spans across the treacherous East River ... and then look at the skyscrapers around it. Without engineers, we'd still be fielding panther attacks in the parlor of our log cabins, as the early settlers.

Two months after Lexington and Concord in 1775, the United States appointed a chief engineer and two assistants. Colonel Richard Gridley was the top man to start with, and he and the other engineers of the Continental Army (including the legendary Polish freedom fighter Thaddeus Kosciuszko and some French engineers later in the war) tackled a daunting range of military problems of the day, chief among them being the defending and attacking of fixed positions, the crossing of large and gnarly bodies of water, and the construction of some decent roads. You can still see a few examples of this in the more remote parts of the colonies, where, to beat the mud, logs were laid sideways to make a "corduroy" road that offered no comfort, but at least the semblance of a steady passage through bog and mire.

To make a defensive position in those days, first they scouted the land and tried to find a safe place that couldn't be shelled too easily—one of the problems with Ticonderoga was that it is overseen by a high hill that made withstanding a siege into an unending nightmare for the defenders. Then they would excavate a suitable series of walls, and made loose baskets out of small branches, which were filled with earth and rocks and set upright one after the other. The truly tidy would lay sod on top of that. The idea was to make a structure that would withstand musket and most cannon fire, but not trap your troops in case they needed to flow out over the top and follow up on an enemy's flight.

But the breakthrough year for combat engineers was 1802, when an actual Corps of Engineers was founded, as well as a military academy at the old fortress of West Point. It was begun as an engineering school, and for years was

169

Decent roads were a prime concern for early American engineers. This is an example of "corduroy" roads which were constructed by laying logs across lanes to cover the bog and mire—they made for very bouncy carriage rides.

the only one in the western hemisphere. In peacetime it was often a West Point engineer who led the way with massive municipal construction, and in wartime it was the engineers from up the Hudson who best understood how to move an army across a landscape, how to map that landscape, and then how to either hole up safely or else attack the weak point of an enemy construction and win the day, as at

The magnificent Col. Henry Knox, a little tubby and bookish, but the man with a plan who got the cannons from Ticonderoga to Boston in the dead of winter using his "Noble Train of Artillery," and thus ejected the British from Beantown the following spring. He ran a bookstore in Boston before the war, and his favorite subject was military history—a shining beacon to other overweight bookworms who dream of making a difference.

Mexico City. They built forts everywhere they could get the funding, such as in Norfolk and New Orleans, and fortified New York Harbor to such an extent that it wasn't attacked from the sea at all after they were done. But of course New York offers many places to place fortifications and develop a deadly crossfire on any invading ship. This led to advances in casemated forts or masonry, using a variation on the old Roman formula for cement. And while they were dauntless and never at a loss in war, it was during peace that the engineers made a howling wilderness into a country where travel and commerce was only restricted by the imagination and cash of the dreamers doing the hard work of making a nation. The canals, roads, and railroads that

171

A lovely view of the "Gibraltar of America," the military school known as West Point, showing the narrowness of the river in the Hudson Highlands, which was why they put a fort and a chain of logs across the river here, and why Benedict Arnold decided this was the plumb prize to give to the British. Storm King Mountain is to the right, and Breakneck Ridge is to the left, with Taurus Mountain in the far background to the left. Some of our best and brightest engineers were trained here.

soon crisscrossed the country were to be the arteries and veins of the new republic, and across and over and through them flowed an amazing flood of humanity, and with them came goods and services that made the vast interior into a world power in a mere 150 years.

When war clouds gathered in 1860 the engineers readily put on uniforms, especially those trained at West Point, and their work aided both sides of the conflict in a variety of ways, from the ever-present need for pontoon bridges to cross various rivers in Virginia, to the first good maps of some parts of the country, and always there was the construction and improvement of roads for the massive armies to get from hither to yon. All the familiar subheadings of combat engineering came up regularly in the American Civil War, from fortifications to sieges, and from railroads to balloons and maps. And precious little of the work was done on a nice day or when things were peaceful. While thrusting six pontoon bridges over the Rappahannock River, the boys in blue were peppered liberally by the

A pontoon bridge over the James River photographed with horse-drawn wagons in 1865. Engineers of the Civil War period were expected to be able to thrust such structures over any old stream or river, no matter how big, and to do so in the face of enemy fire. Depending on the amount of shooting and current of the river, the job could be done as quickly as one day of furious work by dozens of men.

Johnny Rebs on the far bank. Another bridge, close to a half mile long at 2,170 feet, was pushed over the James River in 1864 and was the longest floating bridge constructed for close to eighty years. It makes sense that many of the leaders on both sides were old engineering dweebs from West Point: McClellan, Halleck, and Meade, as well as Lee, Johnston, and Beauregard. The general understanding was that if they were smart enough to do their sums correctly and understand engineering, they wouldn't have too much trouble running an army.

But, as was the case with McClellan, who had a "case of the slows" as Lincoln put it, it was not always true that if you could add and subtract and make fancy drawings, you would necessarily be able to unerringly affect the outcome of a given battle. Human beings are notorious for not reducing to numbers very well, and even the best engineers sometimes make mistakes, as the Space Shuttle program has shown us in our own time. For want of a nail, or an o-ring, entire kingdoms have been lost. And some of the groundbreaking work by the engineers on the Missouri and Mississippi Rivers has come in for criticism. You can't plan for everything, nor is simply building something any guarantee that it will still be there when you get back, as any sandcastle aficionado can tell you.

Be that as it may, engineers have tidy minds, such as Chief of Engineers Henry M. Robert, also known for a handy little booklet called "Robert's Rules of Order," and Hiram H. Chittendon, who opened up Yellowstone National Park by his visionary construction of roads and bridges. And just where to look for them in combat is demonstrated by the fact that the first official U.S. casualties of World War I were two engineers, Sergeant Matthew Calderwood and Private William Branigan, on September 5, 1917. American engineers in that war benefited greatly by the fact that they were trained to grapple with a huge continent at home, and when they got to France they methodically set out to build roads and railroads, enlarge port facilities, and shore up some of the sagging mud trenches of that boggy war. Drainage is always the answer to a watery battlefield, that is unless you want it to be boggy, such as when the Germans flooded large parts of the Cherbourg peninsula prior to D-Day in 1944. The Americans also brought foresters to the Old World, and the 20th Engineers cranked out close to two million feet of lumber in a short time during their stay in France. Engineers were also in charge of the first Yank tanks and the chemical weapons units, which were later spun off into their own branches of service. But the mindset is telling: "Hmmm, wickedly complicated, touchy, difficult … give it to the engineers."

As with so many other facets of American warfare, World War II was a watershed. More money was spent in 1942 to build bases and manufacturing facilities than had been spent between 1920 and 1938, and when the Corps of Engineers was done with their work at home, they could sleep 4.37 million military men in varying degrees of comfort, and had hospital space for 180,000 more. They also slammed up 149 factories to make munitions and build aircraft, and secured a tidy 205 million square feet of storage. They were then free to join the troops and see what needed building and blowing from one end of the world to the other. Along the way they came to be known for dauntless and phlegmatic bravery, and a sneaking suspicion that TNT could solve anything. This isn't quite right, but you can see how you might arrive at that conclusion. Self-taught train-wreckers like Colonel T. E. Lawrence in the Middle East had

One of the clever bits about the planning of the D-Day invasion of Normandy was the fact that there were no suitable large harbors in the target area, as there were at Cherbourg and the Pas de Calais, helping the Germans to not see the Normandy area as a potential invasion spot. To counter this lack, Allied engineers came up with these so-called "Mulberry" units, which were portable floating harbors that could be slammed into place on a beach and provide docking for quite large ships. Here a tug is towing one ashore a few days after the landings.

to make do with their own best guesses, and when he blew his first train, he used much too much dynamite. But they wanted that train to disintegrate—and that's just what Lawrence got, with the pieces raining down upon his men as they sought shelter. "OK ... so maybe just the right amount at just the right place will accomplish the same ends with slightly safer means, what?" If self-made engineers live long enough, often they have a very good grip on the consequences of their actions, and the most economical ways to build or wreck an important place.

Engineers served in every campaign from North Africa to the very end, as civilian engineers were building the bombs that would end the war, and prompt one of them to write in his diary, quoting the Upanishads, "I am become Death..." After a few false starts, combat engineering became a rough science with more than a little art to it. First they had to secure beaches, either by swimming or paddling in ahead of time and wiring the inevitable obstacles with satchel charges, or by going in with the first wave and doing the same thing while the enemy could see them and tried to stop them. The Normandy landings in 1944 were a good example of this, where combat engineers not only opened the beaches, but also used so-called "bangalore torpedoes" (which is an explosive charge on the end of a series of sticks that screw together) to open the land behind the beaches by breaching the barbed wire and many steel obstacles that Rommel had caused to be placed where he deemed them most annoying. Then, once they were ashore, they had to get those roads in good condition—American boys like good roads, and that means wide enough to have a line of trucks and tanks going one way and a similar line coming back the other. This was done with bulldozers and excavators. But in the bocage region just behind the Normandy beaches, the hedgerows provided the enemy with too many places where he could hide and surprise our troops. A young tank sergeant came up with a solution, and a variation is still used today, in the form of Rome ploughs that can uproot and displace almost anything.

During the Battle of the Bulge, December of 1944, everyone was surprised—except the engineers. They had wired many of the bridges in the area with explosives, and managed to blow quite a few of them, giving the attacking Germans fewer options and buying time until the weather cleared and more troops could be rushed up to deal with

The 308th Combat Engineer Battalion is shown here sweeping a snowy road in Belgium circa 1945. Why are they sweeping the sides of the road? Well, there were hardly any combat engineers more clever and experienced than the Germans, and often they would not only rig the road with mines, but also figure that enemy troops would run into those and try to bypass them by taking to the side ditches—and boom.

this rupture in the assault on the Rhine. Blowing up bridges can be accomplished in quite a few ways. You have to ask yourself "Will we be needing to cross this river again?" The answer to that is very often "You bet we will!" So it doesn't pay to make the Lawrence mistake and have the bridge parts fly up over the moon after you rig the wires and push the plunger down firmly on your box several hundred yards away. In the world of combat engineering, you want to make the bridge unusable for a prescribed period of time, and that may mean just taking out a center span, for instance. Even the most reckless tankers aren't going to try to jump the gap.

World War II also featured the legendary Seabees, the construction battalions of the U.S. Navy, and the series of bases they built across the Pacific are still in use. These troops, like all engineers, came mainly from a construction background, but they were also expected to shoot the enemy if he was in sight, and to slam up bases and hospitals and roads and docks and cranes and warehouses at an amazing pace, all of which they did with a smile and the usual profane commentary. They also developed a way to make instant airfields, sometimes overnight, by using sections of pierced-steel planking that fit together like an erector set, and could be laid out by raw muscle in a very short time and still support fighter planes. The U.S. Marine Corps benefited from these forward bases in that their own USMC close air support could be fueled and rearmed as close as five hundred yards behind the island battlefields, and thus provide almost constant harassment of the Japanese defenders. The motto of the Seabees was "Can Do!" and in many years of conflict there have been precious few projects that they couldn't accomplish.

During the Korean War combat engineers once again played a major role, such as in the construction of the defensive positions that delineated the Pusan Perimeter, as well as going up with the troops and assaulting the many fortified hill positions that are such a theme of that conflict. Engineers would do whatever it took to take a strongpoint, be it explosives or flamethrowers, and our troops were always glad to see them because it meant that the professionals had arrived. They could do it all, from emplacing

These men of the 77th Combat Engineer Company are shown during the Korean War, using explosives to blast Chinese troops out of caves and bunkers scattered along the Hantan River. Some of these men may have had experience doing this with Japanese defenders five years earlier on Pacific islands. If they won't come out of the cave with their hands up, this is the recourse you have, because you have got to clear those caves and keep pushing forward—that's the way of it with combat engineers.

and removing minefields, to making a safe haven for food and rest in a combat zone, as well as constructing hasty roads behind the lines that allowed for the shifting of friendly troops laterally to where they were most needed. And always there was the need to make and break bridges as the situation warranted.

In Vietnam their role was the same, and the introduction of the new and improved Rome plough made dealing with the dense undergrowth of that country a little easier. This one had an armored cab for the operator and a new type of blade out front that could not only dig up mines safely and push them aside, but also a special blade for taking out trees. Combat engineers in Vietnam acquitted themselves as they have always done, with valor and ingenuity in the most impossible places.

Today's combat engineer has all the tools that engineers have always carried, from construction to destruction options, and they employ them with the same spirit as their predecessors. They have branched out quite a bit, still helping the national homeland with infrastructure issues, but today they are often called upon to bring first combat capabilities to any American military force, and then to do a fair

One of the legendary "Tunnel Rats" of the Vietnam War, who were volunteers willing to crawl down into one of the thousands of clever tunnels the VC had dug throughout South Vietnam, and there grapple (sometimes hand-to-hand) with enemy soldiers in pitch black smoky darkness. Although this man has an M-16 as well as a gas mask, often the Tunnel Rats had to make do with a Colt .45 M1911, a Kabar knife, and a flashlight.

amount of rebuilding of whatever was wrecked in the preceding hostilities. They have done this in Haiti, Bosnia, Somalia, Iraq, and in many other places scattered around the globe. Their mapmaking is second to none, and their Terrain Analysis Center was one of the deciding factors in the first war with the Iraqi regime. Modern engineering vehicles pushed through the berms and minefields, and then contained the oil fires until private contractors could be called in to contain the many conflagrations.

In Iraq they have struggled in a difficult environment to rebuild the infrastructure, although their efforts have been hampered by an ongoing insurgency that has denied the fruits of these labors to the Iraqi people. Nevertheless, before they went to Iraq, U.S. Army engineers studied cities and towns in America and learned even more about reconstructing an infrastructure such as the sad and sorry one to be found after years of dictatorship in Baghdad. In Iraq, they have also constructed and repaired hospitals, and have even tried to make soccer fields to win over the locals.

Some of their worst work involves dealing with IEDs, improvised explosive devices, which can range from simple grenades to 155mm shells—and that's big enough to blow an M1A1 on its side. There is so much war-junk hanging around in Iraq that it's all but impossible to keep the locals away from it, and while they bear us such ill will it seems that this form of cowardly (but perhaps ultimately effective) guerilla warfare will be appealing to the violent few. American troops have adopted some rough and ready means of dealing with these IEDs, such as parking something heavy in front of them while the rest of the convoy gets by, to training local teams of friendly Iraqis in how to deal with high explosives arranged cunningly to either be

One nightmare from the Gulf War of 1991 that we didn't face in 2003 was the lighting of oil wells from one end of the country of Iraq to the other. These fires were a terrible environmental threat as well as an economic loss, and some of the best "Hell Fighters" from Texas were brought in to extinguish and cap the wells, as well as teach our combat engineers what to do in such a drastic situation.

tripped by the passage of heavy equipment, or to be remotely triggered by such easy-to-get things as garage door openers. There are still massive unguarded piles of artillery shells scattered about the country, although combat engineers have been gathering them and blowing them up as fast as they can rig the C4 and fire it up, always with the traditional cry of explosive workers: "Fire in the hole!" C4, by the way, is a vast improvement over the old nitro glycerine and TNT, in that it is relatively safe until you stuff a fuse in it and trigger the fuse, and as such it has come to be widely used by everyone from the engineers to Special

Forces, who admire its amazing destructive potential. It can be molded into any shape, and this is useful for cutting just certain parts of bridges and structures, as well as for making booby traps and jamming it into hard to fit spaces.

Combat engineers go through a rigorous course of training, and we are told that the majority do not emerge deafened by explosions. Today they must be not only on the cutting edge of technology, from computers to satellites, but also able to think back in time and improvise what they may need in case Home Depot isn't just up the street, as it so often isn't in a combat zone. There are special bridging vehicles now that extend out a telescoping frame that trucks can drive over, but you never know—they may need to

Interestingly, the top general of the U.S. Army said in June of 2004 that the war in Iraq would not be won militarily, but that information and quality of life would play the larger roles. Here we see U.S. Army Corps of Engineers and civilian contractors working to get the power grid up and stabilized by summer, because oddly enough people in deserts are just happier if they have air conditioners in the 120 degree heat.

build a pontoon bridge yet. Today's engineers also have to understand the full panoply of war, because they never know quite what they are going to find or what they might be called upon to do. For this reason they cross-train with many other branches, and keep up-to-date with the latest information, such as how exactly one can place upright and clear one of the new Stryker AFVs—there are approved spots to place rescue cables, and you better know where they are.

The Corps of Engineers continues to undertake projects at home, mostly involving rivers, and while there has been some criticism of their work in containing the Mississippi, nobody else has stepped up with a better plan or spent anything to implement it. While a certain mistrust of engineers has grown up over the years, it seems unlikely that they will run out of projects anytime soon. There will always be minefields to be cleared, and national disasters to prevent or offer assistance in the aftermath of. And because of the nature of warfare, there will always be a call for brave men and women who will go forward and deal with some difficult and dangerous job, be it destruction of obstacles or the construction of a MASH unit in less than twenty-four hours. For these jobs we are fortunate to have people who still answer with the old Seabee's response of "Can Do!"

CHAPTER 9

Peacekeeping Paradox: Military Operations Other Than War

WARFARE AS A concept is both endlessly complex and frightfully simple. You could say the same thing about chess, or fishing, or golf, or investing. With a specific and well-defined objective in mind, use all your resources to achieve that objective while limiting the wastage of those same resources. But somewhere along the line things have gotten much more complicated, so that now you might have wars that don't seem like wars, peace that isn't remotely peaceful, and military operations that would confound Alexander or Frederick the Great. However, as shall be seen, America itself was founded in part on irregular warfare, and there are precious few things new under the sun.

If the enemy would just line up in a given and known location and wear all the same uniforms (preferably in international orange) and wait there for a bit, why, even military historians and car mechanics could advise you how to best deal with them. There could be set-piece battles that make for corking fine graphics with red and blue arrows swooping about, and the outcome would be assured for a nation like the United States that possesses all the training and material needed to fight anyone anywhere on the face of the planet and to crush them. We could begin with our cruise missiles, advance to air strikes and smart bombs, cue the artillery, and then send the infantry and tanks to winkle the other chaps out of their holes. At the end, there would be a clear-cut victory, and we, as the winners, would get to impose whatever rules we thought were good, and have trials to affix blame upon the more beastly of the enemy combatants, and hang them after a bit of pontificating. Then the lumbering forces could go back to their dusty bases and await the next call to action.

You can hardly blame our enemies if they are resistant to this vision of how a war should go. If their only option were to be shelled into oblivion, why wouldn't they cast about for another way of dealing with the gigantic and overwhelming behemoth of American forces? And they wouldn't have to go very far to find some excellent models, and figure out a way to tie us up and make us chase our own tails—for instance, the British forces attempting to capture the arms at Lexington and Concord in April of 1775. What was the British briefing for that mission? "The honest and loyal farmers of Lexington and Concord will welcome us with garlands, and support our efforts to contain the violent insurgency by capturing their flintlocks and ammunition, and hanging their leaders. Then we'll march back to Boston." Unknown to Pitcairn, the British commander, he was at a tipping point in history, and while he thought he was taking part in a "military operation other than war" (MOOTW), he was, in fact, at the very beginning of a war. There had been no end of indicators that preceded that April morning, but the fact that he went with such a light force indicates he thought it would be a walk through.

Americans in settling the New World had a lengthy apprentice period where they engaged the local peoples in a string of wars, and the terrible part was that they were often of a shockingly informal nature, involved the massacre of their own people as well as Native American settlements, often in the dead of a winter's night, and could drag on for years as each side attempted to gain the upper hand while also going about the business of just getting by. Informal warfare was often the order of the day, and atrocities were committed as a matter of course. Emotions ran high, and there was precious little cultural appreciation for the other side, leading to the viewing of the enemy as a subhuman who needed to be slaughtered. After all, the first settlement in Virginia had been wiped out to a man, and the Pilgrims were not long at Plymouth before there came troubles with the Pequot tribe. You could view the first one hundred and fifty years of our history as one long guerilla war, of the LIC (low intensity conflict) variety. Those early farmers learned that trouble could come at any time, and that it was best to have fortified houses and to keep a gun nearby when out working in the fields, because you never knew who would step out of that forest—French officers leading raiding parties from Canada, malicious Mohawks, drunken colonials, scalping parties of whites out looking for money—and what they would do when they emerged. And often the wrong Indian village was attacked, and Indians who were friendly to the settlers would be slaughtered by those too embittered to check anything other than the color of the skin they were perforating with musketballs.

A popular and erroneous notion is that the Americans learned this form of warfare from the Indians and then used it to win the Revolution, but in fact a majority of battles in that war were fought along European lines, with two sides lining up and using flags to rally around as the straight lines went at each other. And while there certainly were irregular forces such as Morgan's Riflemen in the Revolutionary War and Roger's Rangers in the French and Indian War, they were viewed with disdain by professional military men, and doubts were cast upon their abilities to hold a position with the steadfast and phlegmatic stubbornness of so-called "regular" troops. There is a hint of modern warfare in Washington's measured retreats in the early years, when he tried to foster his strength and only give battle when it suited him, knowing that in a straightforward battle he would be creamed. And so we have him retreating from Brooklyn, retreating from Manhattan, retreating across the Hudson, etc. This was absolutely maddening for the British, who knew that if they could just affix the ragtag and bobtail colonials in a killing field, they could wipe the decks with them using their steady regulars. But with an unsettled wilderness to fade into, Washington was able to resist all attempts to draw him to a field of battle that he had not chosen, and the British obligingly kept their eye on the wrong ball, thought they knew the situation better than they did, and tried to fight the war cheaply by not rushing all their troops to the New World. They vastly underestimated the people and culture of the land they were fighting for, and through their contempt for the colonials and lack of sympathy for them, lost one of the crucial wars in all of history. How could they not understand the desire for freedom and autonomy? Well, it's always easy in hindsight to see what the problem was, but at the time they asked all the wrong questions and made up answers that suited themselves while pertaining to nothing rooted in the reality of the situation. The Americans wouldn't fight a pitched battle unless it suited them, and didn't fight fair when they did fight, and were damned bad sports and probably not gentlemen anyway. But they won.

Napoleon's attempt to subjugate Spain in the early 1800s gives us the word "guerilla" for the unspeakable and pinprick attacks that the locals made upon French forces, and the Russian refusal to give battle during the 1812 campaign echoes the clever thinking of the outnumbered. Napoleon couldn't understand that the Russian commanders had no interest in fighting an old-fashioned battle (except at Borodino), and he was equally confounded that the czar wouldn't sue for peace once French forces conquered Moscow. These were full-scale wars, but they didn't behave the way wars were presumed to behave. The British experience in Afghanistan and South Africa had many of the same features: a rowdy and rebellious population who could shoot very well and knew their land better than you did. Why couldn't they see that the British were just trying to bring them semidetached housing and a parliamentary system? Who was so woodenheaded as to not want tea biscuits and Guy Fawkes Day? These were both peacekeeping operations that went seriously awry.

By the end of World War II, the globe had redrawn itself, and the United States emerged as one of three massive forces in world affairs, the other two being the Soviet Union and the People's Republic of China. In due time it became clear that only the United States was a real superpower, and then began the modern wave of MOOTW. We had certainly fought limited battles in places like Nicaragua and along the Chinese rivers in the 1920s and 1930s, but now we were seen as (and saw ourselves as) the world's policemen, despite warning voices sounding in the wings, and the fact that the world often didn't wish to have a policeman, or a country that thought it knew what was best for other people. The French tried for many years to get their colonies in Indochina and Algeria to be settled and peaceful places, but what this translated into was first a series of short, sharp, and violent encounters, and then full-blown guerilla warfare, with small forces of rebels (having the support of the local peoples) refusing to fight pitched battles against European troops, knowing that they could in no way stand up to air strikes and modern artillery in the field for very long. So they fought at night, and hit soft targets, and killed collaborators, and in the end the French had to leave both of those countries, just as they had left Spain a century and a half earlier.

The American experience in Vietnam is a classic case of a peacekeeping mission gone wrong. Because of our fixation on the Domino Theory, we wound up supporting a corrupt regime, killing millions of the enemy, winning every regular military encounter—and having to leave in 1975. The Russians went out of their way to help the Viet Cong, for which we repaid them in full by supporting the Mujahideen in Afghanistan in the 1980s. But note the complexity and interlocking pieces: our support of violent Islamic forces paved the way for the current wars we find ourselves embroiled in fighting. The 1980s also saw us fighting in our

A soldier getting the snow off of an AH-64A Apache attack helicopter near Tuzla in Bosnia in 1997. Peacekeepers have to fly no matter what the weather, have to keep all the gear up and running, and also have to beware of people shooting at them, perform police duties, fix the infrastructure, and make sure everybody gets fed, and ... the list goes on and on.

own hemisphere, in both Grenada and Panama, and neither one was a major war—but they featured all the shooting and risk anyone would expect in a conflict.

With the collapse of the Soviet Union came a time that was both prosperous for the Western world and incredibly dangerous everywhere else. The 1990s became the testing lab for peacekeeping and MOOTW, and it was a hard critter to get a handle on. We were the remaining superpower, and had the men and women and equipment to do things no other country would dream of doing—limited only by our leaders and their ideas of what was the proper way to use an army in a time when there was no large war, but instead a series of small conflicts that were just as dangerous as the artillery of World War I, but without the closure that wars had offered previously.

The record is staggering. In 1990 we evacuated the American embassy in Monrovia, Liberia. The next year we fought Operation Desert Storm, a four-day war using 100,000 of our troops with a mere 110 casualties. We also had to evacuate the American embassy in Somalia. We tried to help the refugees in northern Iraq, at the same time offering humanitarian assistance in Bosnia-Herzegovina. We

An American sergeant handing out presents to orphans in Bosnia illustrates the common decency of our troops, as well as the tragedy of war that made these kids orphans. Will they be throwing rocks at our troops a few years hence? Well, that depends on how well we play the game of perception and PR in that strife-torn land, as well as elsewhere around the world.

193

These soldiers running a vehicle checkpoint in Kosovo have the right idea: get the driver to show you around his car, and watch him like a hawk. Of course, in Kosovo we didn't have anywhere near the problems we have encountered in Afghanistan and Iraq with suicide bombers.

eventually withdrew from Somalia following a botched effort to capture a rebel warlord, but had better luck in Bosnia due to participation from NATO and UN forces. We put troops into Haiti, not for the first or last time, and did relief operations in Africa including Mombassa, Kenya, and Burundi. We ran air strikes in Bosnia, tried to keep the warring factions apart, and conducted combat search and rescue. It was just like a war, but there was no war. We ignored various African genocides, such as the one in Rwanda, because we couldn't figure out if there was any political

194

support for the mission. And we wound up deploying troops to every corner of the globe for a range of missions that were sometimes humanitarian, sometimes linchpins of grand strategy, and sometimes just dirty little conflicts that nobody else would dare meddle in, or have the resources to address. But all of them featured the full spectrum of peace-keeping, meaning that in all of these places there were armed and hostile locals with whom to deal. Could there be a more difficult task to ask of a military force?

And think of the range of skills needed from soldiers who are also expected to rebuild often desperately poor and violent countries. You have to have first-rate language and people skills, excellent intelligence, keep the big picture in mind as you grapple with the day-to-day issues like water and electricity, hand out candy to kids, set up a police force that is credible in the eyes of the locals, fight corruption and injustice, and watch out for snipers and suicide bombers. We always hope that we can graft democracy onto anyplace in the world, including countries and cultures that have never been remotely democratic, but at least that's a good change from our previous policy of supporting right-wing death squads and military dictators simply because they were not communists. The best you can say for MOOTW and the like is that only a truly great nation (or one besotted with hubris) would even think of getting involved.

Consider a simple matter like security. People can't vote and read the newspapers in peace if there are armed insurgents roaming the land. So first, vehicle checkpoints need to be set up and manned with very mature and well-trained soldiers. A good checkpoint has a security team in front of it to spot obvious suicide bombers, a stop sign with barriers and soldiers at the ready, and then a place to actually search

A view of the horrific immediacy of peacekeeping, as Marines scramble through the rubble of their barracks in Beirut searching for missing comrades after a suicide bomber in a truck breached the front gate and detonated a massive explosion. It well shows the high price to be paid in the lives of our most dedicated and patriotic young people.

vehicles. You're going to have to speak their language and know their culture lest your vehicle checkpoint devolve into shooting every ten minutes. You may be able to use closed circuit television to help with some of this, but the experience and training of the commanders and soldiers will ultimately determine how successful your checkpoint is going to be. Cars and trucks need to be stopped in any one of a number of ways, from just waving them down to using concrete barriers and armored personnel carriers, to spraying them with enough full auto bullets to incapacitate the driver. There are no routine stops—every one of them can potentially go wrong, and while you're just having a boring day at a checkpoint, somebody else may be starting a war—remember Major Pitcairn. When searching cars and trucks, a good knowledge of law enforcement issues and mechanical nuance is helpful. You have to look for recent modifications or new paint. Watch the driver at all times, and have them open the trunk or hood. Are they nervous? Is it just because of the stop, or because they have weapons and explosives stashed under the false floor in the trunk? Explosives that can be triggered by remote control, by pres-

The Beirut Memorial outside Camp Lejeune, home of the 22nd and 24th Marine Expeditionary Units, dedicated to the men and women of the USMC who served in Beirut as peacekeepers from August 1982 to February 1984.

sure, by time delay, by being tilted, and in ma y e er ways. Are all the wires under the hood related to combustion engines? Cars are full of small hidden spaces, and mor can be easily made. Under the dash, under the carpet, inside the doors, all are fruitful places for hiding things, as smugglers and terrorists well know.

Or consider how to rebuild the infrastructure of a country. This is everything that makes a place livable from the Western point of view, such as electricity and plumbing. For this engineers are needed who know more than explosives and bridging techniques. Getting a power plant up and running, making sure there is clean water, and getting lights into dark places may take all your troops and all your time—and with an active insurgency, you may need those troops just to run security. Building a local police force is always difficult, because in many parts of the world the police are brutal and corrupt monsters with guns. How will you make sure the locals know you are setting up decent and honest cops? And until you do, your troops will need to be the police force, and prosecute everything from shoplifting to serial killers.

Worst of all is stepping in between two local factions that don't like each other, and in some cases have been pursuing bloody vendettas for centuries. It's sort of like stepping into a fight in a bar—often the two sides will unite against you, not understanding your humanitarian impulses. As much as they don't like each other, they like you even less. To solve this you will need to get everybody to agree to sit down and talk, and sometimes that only happens at the barrel of a gun. But you cannot force people to be reasonable, anymore than you can force them to be peaceful and productive, or not resent the images of America they see on

their televisions every night. You'll have to show them up
ose and personally that you are a good egg, and you are
there to help. And you may have to duck everything from
bricks to RPGs while you're showing them what a great
person you are and how you're really just here to make
things better. And keep in mind that if you stay too long
they will see you as a conquering force, and then the populace will unite with the rebels and the entire country will be
a free fire zone. Ordinary people will cheer your casualties,
and may even commit atrocities, which of course will anger
your troops and encourage them to commit atrocities in
return unless their commanders keep them on a very short
tether. At some point the best thing to do in any MOOTW is
to try to nudge things toward the sort of world you would
like to see, and then leave. Your very presence may be
screwing up the nation-building and peacekeeping process.

Notice how much of this is a humanitarian issue, along
with diplomacy and statecraft, as well as the PR spin that
enables one to manage the perception of a peacekeeping
force. But much of it has to be done by soldiers, and they are
armed and in uniform because the correct assumption is
that there may be violent episodes at any time and in any
location. This also means that you can't just lay out a camp
somewhere; as we learned in Lebanon, the enemy knows
where we sleep at night, and can strike us there with devastating results if we let our guard down. Likewise, convoys
of food and medicine are natural targets for guerillas,
because they can set up ambushes and then slink away, and
they don't care if you're bringing biscuits and plasma to
people who need those things.

T. E. Lawrence had a somewhat simplified way of thinking about the Arab rebellion against the Turks that he

These are men doing the hardest job in the modern world. 1st Lt. Julian Gudger of the USMC (on the right) is shown using a local Albanian translator to ask about a sniper position in Kosovo. Imagine the patience, restraint, and professionalism of men like Lt. Gudger, in an alien culture, representing a foreign power, trying to keep everyone safe while keeping the bad folks on the run. Hats off to them, and Semper Fi!

helped organize in 1917. He estimated that the Turks would need a blockhouse with at least twenty men every four square kilometers to pacify that area, and that this would require 600,000 troops, whereas the Turks only had 100,000 they could throw at the task. This was also part of the early French thinking in Indochina and Algeria, and the result is that you have a safe area near the blockhouse, but then you don't control any of the intervening space—and it is there that the guerillas operate, moving among a friendly population, while you can't even go out for a local meal without getting a grenade in your lap or a stray shot from a high point.

Is there any way to keep peacekeeping from tipping over into guerilla warfare? Well, you'd have to understand the culture forward and backward, know where the traditional fractures and allegiances lay, speak the language, know the folklore, sing the songs, and know the hopes and dreams of the ordinary people. And you'd have to come at them with great compassion and understanding, and see them as different than your troops but in no way inferior, and work like the dickens to get them involved with the remaking of their country. This means finding and supporting moderate leaders that have credibility with the locals, and not just convenient puppets that you jam into place, and trying to do the most good for the largest amount of the population. And even then there will probably be lunatic fringe elements that will try to kill you in your sleep no matter what good you claim to be doing. Might a force other than the military better do some of this? Well, the problem with that is that there is always the chance that it could break out into a full-scale shooting war, and civilians and diplomats are generally at a loss once all hell breaks loose, and represent a liability for the military as they try to deal with the new reality. So the ball goes back to the military forces.

Current doctrine is to use military methods and precautions for all MOOTW, while also emphasizing the diplomatic and social interactions that can make a world of difference in winning the hearts and minds, and trying to have a clear objective and then follow through until that objective is achieved. Naturally, when this gets crossed with civilian leadership, there are some miscarries. In many ways it

201

An MH-53M Pave Low IV helicopter nuzzles up to a refueling drogue during flood relief operations in Central Mozambique in 2000. It isn't any safer doing all this flying and refueling just because it isn't a war.

seems as if the military would like to be left out of such impossible scenarios, arguing that troops are for fighting battles. After all, if all you have is a hammer, everything looks like a nail, and like it needs to be nailed. But today we ask so much more of our troops that we may be seeing either the end of the old military, or the beginning of a new branch of service, or a little of both. The final results are not in just yet. Perhaps after the combat portion of a visit to a foreign land, a new unit could step in right away and attempt to do all the humanitarian and peacekeeping chores, while also having the ability to go back to combat right away if need be? General Krulak of the USMC famously posited the "three block conflict" a decade ago, in which on one block you'd be building schools and setting up elections, while one block away you'd have a sniper and some religious nut in a truck with a bomb, and the next block after that would be full-scale combat with jets swooping in off aircraft carriers and M1A1 tanks racing around the landscape. He thought it was all a possibility, and in just such a tight space.

Also, keep in mind that simply operating the military establishment in peacetime is a dangerous job. There's too much driving and flying around in bad weather, and too much fuel, and too many things to coordinate. Be that as it may, any large endeavor contains many of the same dangers, and the answer has always been training and leadership. There are safe ways to cross rivers and fly jets, and the military knows what they are as well as any segment of society. The issues of having an objective and then maintaining security will never change, but you need that in peace as well as in war. One of the crucial things needed for MOOTW is the notion of restraint, and this takes a little more work to emplace in the military mind. To appreciate the value of restraint, you'd have to be looking at the big picture, and realize that while a violent and rapid response to a situation may solve your immediate problem, it may well cause trouble out of all proportion to the action itself if it is spun that way by your own or the enemies' media. A classic example of this is the use of religious buildings for sniping and rocket attacks. If you just stay there and let them do this to you, you're not making progress, but if you flatten the mosque or church, you are digging yourself a hole with the local people that may have no way out. What's the right answer? We're still trying to find it. It might be excellent snipers with night vision capability and audacious penetrative abilities, or it might be Special Forces sneaking in and cleaning house, or it might be a precision strike from a guided weapon that can minimize damage. Any way you do it, there's going to be some problems, so the decision is which of them is the one you can best deal with.

Likewise with intelligence operations, which can be your greatest friend and worst liability in peacekeeping. Do you really want to set up a country where everyone is informing on a neighbor? Do we want the United States to be like that? Following 9/11, it hasn't always been clear just where we stand on this issue. And what about an assassination program, where enemy leaders and operatives would be killed with little fanfare? We tried that in Vietnam, and Operation Phoenix didn't seem to give us the traction we thought it would, despite the twenty to thirty thousand Vietnamese that were killed by either being shot or thrown out of helicopters. What makes for the best intelligence in support of military and peacekeeping objectives? Let's go back to knowing a country and its culture, respecting the traditions and trying to understand the lifestyles and historic problems, and then flooding it with our people who speak their language and can commiserate about draught and goat herding if those are issues.

MOOTW asks more of us as a country and more of our military than any other sort of task we could undertake. It asks us to grapple with thorny and complex issues that are often not black and white, and to make a mature and measured plan that can be carried out in a realistic time frame by a force that is sometimes ill-prepared to come to grips with something more subtle than shooting and bombing. Childish rhetoric and intemperate leadership will promote instability. Unilateral military moves smack of the actions of

A modern-day Braveheart, Lt. General William Wallace is shown here giving his men a pep talk, which included the sage advice to be on their guard in Iraq, and to "Show the people of this country the proper respect, but be careful. There's still a bunch of knuckleheads running around," as the mission changed into a peacekeeping and humanitarian phase. Leadership hasn't changed much over the years, and leaders like this are worth their weight in gold as America's missions grow in scope and complexity.

a petulant teenager, and as such have no place in world leadership. The very best part of our nature has to be drawn out of the troops on the ground, and it has to appeal to the people we are trying to help. Often this will not be our exact vision of how things ought to be. But we might begin by finding the very best thinkers and writers of a given country, and see what they have to say. Our policies might be a clever restatement of such national thoughts. And then we have to drill our troops again and again to stand in the middle of two mobs throwing rocks at each other, and always happy to team up and throw some at them. We need to try to think the way the locals do, and ask ourselves "What would I do if an army occupied America and claimed they wanted to stabilize our nation and help us out?"

The hope behind every peacekeeping and humanitarian mission is that everyone around the world is more alike than different, and mostly what they want is a decent job and a family in a home with water and the chance to explore the amazing and fun parts of life. And the United States, through a commitment to democracy and peace, is actually willing and able to send in a force that can give people some breathing room from oppression, and in the best case help nudge them towards freedom. The paradox of peacekeeping is that it involves so much shooting. The task, from a military point of view, is as elite and difficult as any in our past, from Saratoga to Gettysburg to The Marne and Tarawa—and yet we have never flinched before when it came time to oppose oppression and take a stand for decency and the rule of law, at home and abroad. Now, however, the challenge today is to not just violently oppose injustice, but to also use peaceful means to support our objectives, even if that means keeping a rifle nearby—because after all, just as in colonial America, you never know who is going to step out of those woods.

CHAPTER 10

Secret Warfare: The Lure of Daring

WHAT COULD BE more pulse pounding? They're five minutes out, inbound, moving at over 100 mph just above the landscape in a blacked-out helicopter, part of a small team that is about to touch down and commence a secret military mission. Everyone is armed to the teeth, trained and honed into twelve men with one mind, using the latest in real-time communications and GPS, and on their way to pull off something that an entire army couldn't do as well or as quickly. The odds are long, but spirits are high. These are the best soldiers the world has ever seen, not just at a level beyond physical fitness, but more seasoned, more intelligent, better-trained, speaking more languages, and able to smack down anybody they run across, or call in air strikes and artillery to back their play, unless they mean to hand out $100 bills and start training the locals to mount an insurgency. They don't look like weight lifters; instead, they are mostly long and lean, verging on wiry, and they tend to have a certain twinkle in their eye

207

All Special Forces are now under the command of Special Operations Command, which saves a lot of time and effort rebuilding the wheel in each service, and spreads the assets around where they will do the most good. Larger than most country's entire armies, there are about 45,000 special warriors ready to go at any time.

and a grand sense of humor—among themselves, that is. Outsiders are not welcome.

They all are cross-trained so that any given member of the team can take on two or three other roles should the situation warrant it, and they all have clearances above top secret because they have to look at a lot of classified briefing data and liaise with spooks, criminals, fanatics, weirdos, assets, liabilities, warlords, drug runners, terrorists, religious nuts, refugees, wannabe heads of state, and remote villages of old men, women and children—and they have to have a slightly different approach to each of these individuals. This is the modern world of Special Operations, and it is the day-today reality for the men (and some women) of the CIA's paramilitary, U.S. Navy SEALs, U.S. Air Force Special Operations, U.S. Army Special Forces, Delta Force, USMC Force Recon, and the shadowy operatives of Gray Fox, Task Force 5, Task Force 20, and Task Force 121. The work they do is secret and ongoing, and runs the gamut from just a little bit secret all the way to Black Ops that are even sometimes believably and plausibly deniable.

Maybe it's best if we don't know. And yet, there is a rational point of view based on long experience with Special Operations and clandestine military actions that argues it causes more trouble than it solves, costs a great deal of money, is hard on the soldiers involved, and doesn't really achieve the ends we would wish in the larger picture. But those voices are muted right now—there is no McGeorge Bundy to describe the run-up to and fallout from the Bay of Pigs fiasco. In the current environment we are witnessing an explosion of secret war on a scale unseen since World War II, and it's easy to figure out why.

After September 11, 2001, the gloves came off. In just a few weeks our Special Forces were inside Afghanistan and on the hunt. The political will was there, and the teams were ready. There was no lack of daring, from the top on down, and there has been precious little thought given to anything other than giving these secret operatives as much money and as much support as they need to do things that would make the average civilian pass away from fright. And in the wake of the attacks on the United States, a lot of things seemed like a good idea that may not be a good idea in the cold light of history—such as the wishful thinking that tried to prove a tie between Al Qaeda and Iraq. But perhaps we've gotten ahead of ourselves.

Throughout history there have always been spies, but the idea of secret war is a relatively new one. Irregular forces such as Roger's Rangers did indeed pave the way for some of this mentality, but it wasn't until World War II that secret war came to seem like not just a stop-gap notion, but an actual branch of thought and way of operating that promised great results by the actions of a few. It was economical, had a demonstrable impact, and harkened back to the daring of people like Leatherstocking and the Scarlet Pimpernel. In some ways it was a philosophical turn in military history, in that the primacy of the individual came to the fore above and beyond the sweep of mighty armies and massive navies. One man could make a difference, by working with partisans from China to Yugoslavia, by parachuting into occupied Norway and France, and by blowing bridges and attacking sentries. American author Ernest Hemingway captured the feeling of this kind of war perfectly in his novel *For Whom the Bell Tolls*, in which the idealistic American teacher Robert Jordan links up with a group of peasant guerillas during the Spanish Civil War, his job being to use his engineering and special operations background to blow a bridge at just the right time to prevent reinforcements from coming over that river. All across the globe, from Europe to Asia, the men and women of such organizations as SOE (British) and OSS (American) fought just such secret wars, not because they needed to stay out of the limelight, but because of the gap between the threat posed by the Axis and the response of the mighty arsenals of democracy. Before millions of American troops and thousands of airplanes and tanks could roll onto the European continent and a bloody progression of Pacific islands, short sharp actions were being fought in hills and towns around

The famed Alamo Scouts of World War II, were Super Rangers who accomplished the only successful large-scale rescue mission of the war by means of stealth and overwhelming combat skills. Note the mix of camouflage, including USMC-issue jungle style, and the preference for the Thompson submachine gun, which, while it was heavy, packed a goodly wallop and was handy in the jungle.

the planet. The work was dangerous to the highest degree, and frustrating, but at least action was being taken. It should be noted, however, that it took gigantic armies and considerable casualties to actually win the war—commandos, however brave they were, couldn't do it on the cheap. But this was also the golden age of Special Forces in every army involved, from the German Brandenburgers and their elite and savage SS, to the Russian naval commandos, to the American paratroopers, Rangers, Marines and frogmen, to the British SAS, SBS, and commando teams.

In the years following World War II a so-called "Cold War" began, and it was here that secret war got going, particularly in the United States and Soviet Union. The 1947 charter of the CIA contains a funny little clause allowing for "certain other functions," and depending on your point of view, this was

211

either the start of a deal with the devil, or the commencement of a glorious time when actions could be taken without a lot of tiresome debate in Congress. The CIA was supposed to be a tweedy little outfit that gathered and analyzed intelligence—and that's it. Instead of that, the men and women of OSS brought their wartime experiences and mentality with them into the Cold War, and launched a series of strikes that they reckoned would pave the way for later actions. Unfortunately, the first batch of ops failed big time. Of the teams dropped into, say, Albania, all of them were caught and either imprisoned or executed. Then we trained hundreds of Tibetans in Colorado and parachuted them into their home country to smite the Chinese—and the vast majority of them were cut off without sufficient backup and slaughtered almost to a man.

Interestingly the regular military leadership didn't like these spooks and secret warriors all that much. Too much chutzpah, too many cowboys, irregular uniforms, lack of oversight and chain of command, weird little missions, and asking soldiers to do patently insane things like drop into the Soviet Union and blend in. Try blending into a foreign country sometime. You'll make fifty mistakes in your first hour, and in the case of most of these missions, there wasn't a second hour to hone your skills as an Albanian peasant. But there were some successes—in the short term, that is. In Guatemala we backed a regime that ousted the pesky Reds, and never mind if they slew their fellow countrymen with impunity. In Iran we sent Kermit Roosevelt on Operation Ajax, where he was able (with considerable sacks of money) to organize riots and put our man in place. Unfortunately, "our man" was the Shah of Iran, and by the time the people rose up and ousted him his brutal secret service and lunatic army had fostered so much hate for him and his American backers that we're still dealing with the fallout. The list goes on and on.

Perhaps the passage of years can help us strike a balance in thinking about these secret missions. There can be no doubt that the bravery and ingenuity of the men at the sharp end of the stick was beyond belief. These were heroes, and there is no debating the hard choices and tremendous risks they took on our behalf. And, after all, the dang Russians were doing the same thing anyplace they could get a foothold, from Cuba to Angola to Vietnam. If there is anyone who should be called to task for some of the things that happened, like the assassination of leaders we didn't like, or the subversion of elections, it is the men at the top of the political and intelligence realms. That's where the buck stops. But even there we have a few oddities, such as the CIA unhelpfully guessing that if the president really didn't know about an operation, well, there was no political fallout that could come home to roost in any given November, right? Thus we have Mr. Dulles laying out the Bay of Pigs for the young Jack Kennedy, who thought it sounded all right. The word was that the Cuban people would rise up when their own anticommunist forces hit the beaches and throw that rascal Castro out on his ear. What Mr. Dulles left out of those briefings was the fact that an amphibious force with no air cover didn't stand much of a chance on those beaches, and there would be no popular uprising, and that we had been dealing with American Mafia figures to mount at least seven assassination attempts against Castro.

But along with his youth and his father's fortune, Kennedy had a taste for secret war, and it was he who got the Green Berets and Navy SEALs off the ground, and there was a strange link between these forces and the world of the CIA.

Sometimes men from elite units would just be used as they were, and sometimes they would be "sheep-dipped," meaning the records showed that they had resigned from the military, but oddly enough they were still fighting overseas. There was the illusion that a concept known as "plausible deniability" would protect American politicians from a lot of bad comments as they pontificated at the United Nations and in other public venues. But whom did we fool? Just ourselves, as it turns out. You couldn't actually talk about choice and freedom and democracy and then turn around and fight dirty little secret wars while supporting corrupt fascists just because they weren't communists without consequence.

But that didn't stop us from trying, and there is a crucial lesson in that. The men who waged these wars really thought they were doing the right thing, and a desperate struggle with a deadly enemy justified any means, including assassinations, the slaughter of civilians, and the support given to leaders who, if they weren't strange Third World versions of Hitler and Mussolini, were drug and crime lords at home in their spare time—or all of the above all the time. You can trace some of this back to a secret report that the CIA asked General Jimmy Doolittle to conduct during the early 1950s. Why weren't our covert actions going the right way? Doolittle concluded that we needed to put the kibosh on "traditional American notions of fair play," and that if we just got down and dirty with the enemy, and used some of their terror tactics, we would come out on top. The ends would justify the means. The fact that traditional American notions of fair play were one of the bright shining beacons ever kindled on the planet in 10,000 years of warfare and misery was overlooked, and all but given up. The secret wars ground on, far from the spot-

SEAL Team One deploying along the Bassac River in South Vietnam in 1967. The SEALs are still pretty darn good at secret war, and can rig up almost anything that floats with a motor and tear off on a recon with very little lead-time. If they mean to gather information, you won't even hear them, and if they mean to cause you trouble, you'll be in a world of hurt.

light, in places like Vietnam and Laos and the Congo and South America. Extraordinary individuals rose up through the ranks of the traditional military, and were then taken aside and asked if they'd like to serve in another way, a more exciting way, than just going through a service career that was dull and predictable in peacetime. And the best of them, the most intelligent and idealistic, did indeed enter that dark world.

Take MACV-SOG. This was the Military Assistance Command Vietnam Studies and Observation Group. Pretty prosaic name, right? Never exceeding about two thousand men, SOG ran cross-border operations from the central highlands of Vietnam into Laos and Cambodia in an attempt to shut down the Ho Chi Minh Trail, which was the foot and truck path that enabled the North Vietnamese to move men and equipment down to where they could make incursions on South Vietnam. Operating in small teams of two or three Americans and perhaps six or seven local troops, the men of SOG did the most hair-raising missions that have ever been recorded. They were always outnumbered, operating in a country where they were not supposed to be, trying to stop a tremendous flow of arms and enemy soldiers on a pathway through the trackless hills and forests and jungles of a remote land, and their adventures were such that you have to read them for yourself to fully appreciate the dauntless courage and unflagging spirit of these American heroes. They were sneaky when they needed to be, and unbelievably aggressive if the stuff hit the fan. SOG usually went in riding helicopters, and making false landings before getting off at their real destination. Then there would be a pause while the helicopter continued with more false landings, and then the team would move out for anything from a day to a week behind enemy lines, usually where they couldn't be backed up very well by air strikes or artillery. They took pictures, planted sensors, recorded truck and bicycle traffic, and once, when the dweebs in Saigon didn't believe the North Vietnamese were using elephants for transport, SOG troopers brought back a bag of elephant dung and dumped it on their desk—analyze this.

The average SOG was a formidable force to be reckoned with, and the best of them became legends. They all had their own style, from aggressive straight shooters to more thoughtful and ruminative commandos, but everyone who ran those missions undertook a secret war at the behest of the president and in our names, and they acquitted themselves with both honor and glory, and in this case those are not hollow words. But they did all this at a high price, because once the NVA cracked wise to what was going on, there were epic chases and narrow escapes and some of the most savage little combats ever fought. An SOG man carried a Colt Commando, a short version of the M16, and usually about twenty clips to go with it, as well as smoke and explosive grenades, claymore mines, knives, pistols, silenced weapons, and a little food and a tarp to sleep under and some water and a radio—and that was it. More often than you would have any reason to believe they got all their guys out after accomplishing their mission under these most dangerous and difficult conditions. But they also lost many men, sometimes entire teams.

An inherent part of the high price they paid was the fact that they were fighting a secret war, meaning that medals and casualties could simply fall off the table, and men like Sergeant Jerry "Mad Dog" Shriver could last be seen charging a tree line firing his weapon—and then be heard of no more, forever. Why did it have to be secret? Well, we were locked in a diplomatic dance where all sides claimed that Laos was neutral, while in reality it was being used by all sides as an adjunct to the war in Vietnam. So we had the North Vietnamese trundling through there night and day chasing after their goals in South Vietnam, while American forces secretly patroled and bombed and fought actions every step of the way, and meanwhile the CIA was running their own secret war to the west out of Thailand and Laos using Air America, their very own airline, as well as paramilitary troops being led by men like Tony Poe—and all of this supposedly to be out of the spotlight. The result is a bittersweet and tragic chapter in American military history where it is possible to have the highest admiration for the soldiers on the ground, and some pretty pronounced loathing for the civilian leadership who expended our very best men in a war we could not win, in a country that didn't want our help. When all of this broke out in public it ignited a division of the country that has not been resolved to this day, and anger in the White House at the leaks that made all this public began the slide toward Watergate that removed a president because of his desire to cover up a secret war.

So you'd think all that blood and trauma would be a pretty clear lesson, right? Uh, well, no, actually. A mere ten years after Vietnam we were back in the secret war game, this time in Nicaragua and Afghanistan. Once again secret warriors roamed the earth with bags of cash and explosives, this time under Bill Casey of the CIA, an old OSS hand, who authorized worldwide monkey business at a pace to stagger the imagination, while an amiable and befuddled president acted as if he were leading us, and his vice president was "out of the loop"—let's go back to plausible deniability, shall we? And what did we get for those "certain other actions"? Iran-Contra on the one hand, where rogue agents and secret plans emanated out of the office of a fellow who has been called "a marine lieutenant colonel with five stars," and the arming of the Mujahideen, including a chap named bin Laden. It did hasten the fall of the Soviet Union, but it also gave us a lawless area of Afghanistan and Pakistan where we still can't go.

We won the Cold War, mostly by outspending the enemy, and then were propelled in 2001 into the secret wars of the future. Russia is a shambling wreck, but still dangerous, China is a massive country on the brink of democracy, Vietnam is a desperately poor backwater where they're still removing our mines and now would like our tourist dollars, and the enemy today are cells of religious fanatics who

218

hate us so much they are willing to kill themselves to knock down our buildings and kill our civilians.

Fortunately, after the failed bid to rescue the hostages in Iran following the ouster of the Shah in 1980, U.S. Special Operations remade itself into Special Operations Command, based in Florida. Now each branch of the services has their own commandos, and their own dedicated air wing to move them around, and a seat at the table when missions are being planned. After the near-debacle of Grenada and the somewhat better luck of Panama and Bosnia in the 1990s, by October of 2001, while the rubble at Ground Zero was still smoking, we had the men and policies that would allow us to have global reach and immediate results. But some of the same issues keep coming up. We aren't supposed to be operating in Yemen, and yet when one of the architects of the bombing of the USS *Cole* was out for a spin under the watchful eye of a Predator drone, he got a couple of Hellfire missiles through the sunroof to remind him of the anger of America. We were all over Afghanistan before we sent in regular troops, and bought as many friends there as we could find—although now that the opium crop has shot through the roof, and the country is still not secure, have we just made ourselves a source of future trouble? Then we got pulled off the hunt for bin Laden by civilian leadership who thought we should wade into Iraq since we were having an outing that the American public would approve of—for a while. Our secret warriors did their usual fine job, and managed to kill Saddam's beastly sons and capture the big guy himself in a hole in his hometown—but we're now left with a country that refuses to be pacified and grateful. Turns out they like us less than the lunatic who used to run the place.

There's a curious tension that's always at work here, in that the men in uniform try to do what the folks back in Washington seem to want done, but often the two missions cannot be made to marry up neatly. There is no finer force of covert operators than the one we now have in the field. There are about 50,000 Special Forces all told, and their budget for 2005 seems to be about $6 billion, and that's amazing in that it indicates just how well we understand the importance of these men. The CIA runs about four hundred paramilitary operatives, and these days they work easily and happily with Special Forces, and in some cases make for a fine team. There is still some lingering resentment from the regular military, but more and more often you'll notice that the higher ups at the Pentagon have Ranger tabs and Airborne wings, just one indicator that they know and appreciate the value of elite training.

That training hasn't gotten any easier for our secret warriors over the years. It is as tough and uncompromising as anything you could ask someone to volunteer for, and it emphasizes being able to think on your own, and to behave with a maturity and professionalism that is meant to eliminate some of the old cowboy mentality. The men and women who are fighting in the dark for us now realize that what they do in a small village may have repercussions around the world in an age of digital cameras and twenty-four-hour news cycles. At the same time they are more than ready to shoot from the hip and kill as many enemy soldiers as they can get a clear bead on. There is also the realization that secrets may not stay secret forever. This acts as a powerful brake on many of the abuses of the past, at least from the soldier's point of view.

But is it worth it to fight anywhere secretly? It may be that

A Green Beret of the 3rd Special Forces Group is shown here through a night-vision device as he prepares to do battle with the enemy in Afghanistan. Such secret warriors have a long history of daring actions since they came into their own in World War II, and especially after the role of Special Forces was expanded and sanctioned following the failed rescue at Desert One in 1980.

if it is worth fighting for or about something, the only thing to do in a democracy is to concede some of the surprise and sneaky advantage and have a debate about it, and maybe even a vote. We are currently running a massive secret war in Colombia with very little fanfare, and this despite the fact that we have troops on the ground, have been training Colombian forces at Forts Benning and Bragg, have lost CIA operatives in the field, and may have participated in the killing of Pablo Escobar, the notorious drug lord.

Not a few historians have concluded that secret wars

221

don't work very well, that they create more problems than they solve, and that they are never really secret—somebody is going to blow the whistle sometime. There is no debate that we have the men and money to run such operations, and to do them as well as they have ever been done, and that Special Forces and CIA paramilitary teams are right now doing valuable work all over the globe. These troops are as far from unhappy conscripts as it is possible to get—they are proud volunteers, trained to a fare-thee-well, and have more brains and more combat skills than any soldiers who have ever walked the earth—but is this really the best use of people who are that smart and capable? What if those same teams built schools and dams and factories and housing, taught people to read and think for themselves, upheld human rights and dignity, enforced governments that were free of corruption and worked at the people's command, and operated out in the open? We may never know. But when you're thinking about secret war, think back on Doolittle's advice, and ask yourself why decency and democracy should have to cloak themselves in secrecy? Task Force 121 is evidently getting back in the saddle after their little diversion in Iraq, and it is to be hoped that if any-one can capture or kill bin Laden it will be the amazing men and women of America's Special Forces, probably fighting in secret once again—because they're not supposed to be "over the fence" in Pakistan, and that's probably where the tall man is hiding right now. Well—it's not as if we haven't done this sort of thing before.

Afterword

IN TODAY'S WORLD there is a great gap between the United States military and the public they serve. Past generations of Americans have had the experience of participating in war, but today, the vast majority of adults have had very little military experience and their understanding of military operations, other than what they can glean from movies and books and the nightly news, is wrong and wrong-headed.

Hopefully the preceding chapters have helped expand your understanding of our modern American military machine, and reminded us to consider carefully when and how our vast resources should best be expended in order to achieve our national goals. And we've seen that history offers us some cause for reflection. If we're going to be fighting in cities, will we remember all the difficulties of urban warfare? If we're going in over a beach, will we remember the challenges of amphibious landings? Have our commanders considered the blend and mix of the troops available, and kept the combat engineers at the ready with their fuse-crimping pliers? With all of our armed forces' mobility, can we still get to where we need to get quickly and effectively? Is military intelligence effective? Is sniping the answer to our battlefield problems? And what about peacekeeping? It often sounds like a great idea, but is it really more often an open-ended shooting gallery with our troops in the middle? It's best to remember all of this when the big whistle blows and Americans in uniform are placed in harm's way.

In today's world, special warfare will not always be fought by specialized troops trained for specific operations in their area of specialty, but rather by any soldiers who find themselves in operations where they need special combat skills. Although the Marine Corps specialized in amphibious landings, D-Day was an army and navy operation. Although we have the 10th Mountain Division, most troops today will need to assault hills and mountains at some point in their deployment. We can't train every soldier to do everything that may be required, so the best we can do is make sure their commanders know something of all these forms of special warfare, and that special warfare is pursued in a way that is likely to achieve military objectives in the shortest amount of time and the least loss of life.

Despite the wishes of think tanks and national leaders, warfare is never going to be anything other than an imprecise business that, by its very nature, encourages violence and includes many, many dead bodies. Some will be ours, and some will belong to an enemy force, and some will be civilians who have the unhappy fate of living where war is fought. As such it is important that we, as civilians, do a couple of things right now, today.

The first is to increase our support of our troops. This means speaking kindly to anyone in uniform that you run across, and making sure they have the pay and benefits they deserve for their duties, and it also means getting them the Kevlar vests and armored Humvees they need if they are going somewhere dangerous on our behalf. Another thing we can do is to engage in meaningful conversation about what it means when we unleash all of our special warriors to pursue every facet of the modern military arts. Read everything you can get your hands on concerning all sides of a conflict, and then go back in history and review how warfare works, and then, dare to keep talking.

It's all too easy to become immersed in the ins and outs of war, and to forget the very human price that has to be paid in terms of shattered bodies and minds and landscapes. Yes, there are wars that need to be fought. But conflicts like Vietnam and Iraq remind us why our soldiers are the very best people we have, and how hard it is to thrust them into a killing field for no very good reasons. We ignore the voices of those soldiers at our peril. In our review of the various forms of special warfare, let's always try to remember the larger picture, because, in the end, what we want is not war, but peace. The very best soldiers and leaders know this, and we should remember it as well. As Colonel Robert Gould Shaw of the 54th Massachusetts said, "We fight for men and women whose poetry is not yet written." And we should dare to have the decency of General Grant who, after four years of savage fighting, handed back to Robert E. Lee his sword following the surrender at Appomattox—that's the American way.

Bibliography

Air Land Sea Application Center. *Survival, Evasion and Recovery: Multiservice Procedures for Survival, Evasion and Recovery.* Washington, D.C.: Government Printing Office, 1999.

Banks, Arthur. *A World Atlas of Military History, 1861-1945.* New York: Da Capo Press, 1978.

Bartlett, Lt. Col. Merril L., USMC (ret). *Assault From the Sea: Essays on the History of Amphibious Warfare.* Annapolis, MD: Naval Institute Press, 1983.

Brisard, Jean-Charles and Guillaume Dasquie. *Forbidden Truth: US-Taliban Secret Oil Diplomacy and the Failed Hunt for Bin Laden.* New York: Thunder's Mouth Press, 2002.

Cacutt, Len, ed. *Combat: Armed and Unarmed Combat Skills from the Official Training Manuals of the World's Elite Military Corps.* Secaucus: Chartwell Books, 1988.

Chandler, David, ed. *Dictionary of Battles: The World's Key Battles from 405 BC to Today.* New York: Henry Holt & Company, 1988.

Chapman, F. Spencer. *The Jungle is Neutral.* New York: W.W. Norton & Company, 1949.

Crawford, Steve. *Deadly Fighting Skills of the World.* New York: St. Martin's Press, 1997.

Dunnigan, James F. and Albert A. Nofi. *Dirty Little Secrets: Military Information You're Not Supposed to Know.* New York: William Morrow, 1990.

Gilbert, Adrian. *Sniper: The Skills, the Weapons and the Experiences.* New York: St. Martin's Paperbacks, 1996.

Goodenough, Simon. *Tactical Genius in Battle.* New York: E.P. Dutton, 1979.

Halberstadt, Hans. *NTC: A Primer of Modern Land Combat.* Novato, CA: Presidio Press, 1989.

Headquarters, U.S. Air Force. *Search and Rescue Survival Training.* New York: Barnes & Noble Publishing, 2003.

Headquarters, U.S. Army. Training Circular No. 90-6-1: *Military Mountaineering*. Washington, D.C.: Department of the Army, 1976.

Headquarters, U.S. Army. U.S. Army Field Manual 100-5: *Fighting Future Wars*. Washington, D.C.: Brassey's (US), 1994.

Headquarters, U.S. Army. TC 23-14: *Sniper Training and Employment*. Washington, D.C.: Department of the Army, 1989.

Hughes-Wilson, Col. John. *Military Intelligence Blunders*. New York: Carroll & Graf, 1999.

Kayworth, Alfred E. and Raymond G. Potvin. *The Scalp Hunters: Abenaki Ambush at Lovewell Pond—1725*. Wellesley, MA: Branden Books, 2002.

Keegan, John. *Intelligence in War: Knowledge of the Enemy from Napoleon to Al-Qaeda*. New York: Alfred A. Knopf, 2003.

Kennedy, Col. William V., Baker, Friedman and Miller. *Intelligence Warfare: Today's Advanced Technology Conflict*. New York: Crescent Books, 1983.

Kock, H. W. *The Rise of Modern Warfare, 1618–1815*. London: Bison Books, 1981.

Kurland, Michael. *The Spymaster's Handbook*. New York: Facts On File, 1988.

Liddell Hart, B. H. *Strategy*. New York: Penguin Books USA, 1991.

Mitchell, Col. Joseph B. *Decisive Battles of the American Revolution*. St. Simon's Island, GA: Mockingbird Books, 1982.

Plaster, John L. *Secret Commandos: Behind Enemy Lines with the Elite Warriors of SOG*. New York: Simon and Schuster, 2004.

Prados, John. *President's Secret Wars: CIA and Pentagon Covert Operations from World War II Through Iranscam*. New York: William Morrow, 1986.

Purcell, L. Edward and Sarah J. Purcell. *Encyclopedia of Battles in North America, 1517-1916*. New York: Checkmark Books, 2000.

Sledge, E.B. *With the Old Breed: At Peliliu and Okinawa*. Novato, CA: Presidio Press, 1981.

Spicer, Mark. *Sniper: The Techniques and Equipment of the Deadly Marksman*. Miami, FL: Lewis International, 2001.

Tanner, Stephen. *Epic Retreats: From 1776 to the Fall of Saigon*. Rockville Centre, NY: Sarpedon, 2000.

227

Index

AAAVs, 66
Afghanistan, war in, 32, 50, 51, 94, 209, 218, 219
Alexander the Great, 29, 30, 75
Amphibious warfare history of, 53–65
    perils of, 55–56
    present-day strategies for, 65–72
Ancient history, military, 28, 32–33, 53–55, 74–77, 121–123, 165–166, 167
Arnold, Benedict, 33–34, 57

Bacomb, Willard, 62
Baghdad, 3, 23–25
Bosnia, 193, 194
Britain; British, 190
    in ancient times, 33–34
    in American Revolutionary War, 11, 12, 102, 124, 189–190
    in colonial America, 34, 55
    in Napoleonic Wars, 78, 103–104
    in World War I, 59–60, 84–85, 106
    in World War II, 39–40, 132

C4, 183–184
camouflage, 18, 114–116
Cavalry
    equine, 74–84
    history of, 73–87
    mechanized, 84–94
CIA, 132, 135, 211, 213, 217, 218
CIA's paramilitary, 209, 222
Civil War (American), 7, 12, 34–36, 59, 80–82, 104–106, 125–126, 144–145, 172–174
Cold War, 211–218
Colonial America, v–vi, 34, 187–189
Combat engineers, importance of, 164–165
    throughout history, 165–181
    present-day, 181–185
Combat Search and Rescue (CSAR), 147, 148–150, 151–163,
Corps of Engineers, 169–170, 175–185

D-Day, 63–64, 131, 175, 177
Delta Force, 112, 209
Donovan, William J. "Wild Bill," 131–132, 133

Doolittle, Jimmy, 214
Dulles, John F., 213

Engineers, combat. See combat engineers

Ferguson, Patrick, 102, 103
France; French, 191
    in Napoleonic wars, 6–8, 78
    in World War I, 8

Gallipoli, 59–60, 61
Germany; Germans
    in World War I, 8, 36–37, 108
    in World War II, 8, 10–11, 12–14, 40, 85, 110–111, 132
Gettysburg, battle of, 35–36
Gray Fox, 209
Green Berets, 213

Hannibal, 30
Helicopters, use of in military, 17, 65, 86–87, 88, 93, 159–161, 202, 216
Indian Wars (U.S.), 33, 58–59, 82–83, 188–189
Iran, 212–213
Iraq War (1991), 91, 182, 193

Iraq War (2003–04), 23–25, 91–92, 182

Jackson, Stonewall, 34–35
Japan; Japanese, in World War II, 13–14, 109–110, 120–121, 145
Julius Caesar, 30

Kennedy, John, 213
Knox, Colonel Henry, 33, 168, 171
Korean War, 41–42, 64, 135, 147, 179–180

Landing craft, 62–63, 65–66
LCACs, 65–66, 68

M1A1, 88
MacArthur, Douglas, 64
MACV-SOG, 215–217
Marines. See U.S. Marine Corps
Medieval history, military, 77–78
Mexican-American War, 12
Military intelligence history of, 121–135
in World War II, 129–134
present day, 136–140
MOOTW, 188, 191–206
Mountaineering, civilian, 37–39

Mountain warfare equipment for, 47, 49
history of, 28–43
training for, 40–41, 43–51
MOUT, 2
Murat, Marshal Joachim, 78–79

Napoleon; Napoleonic Wars, 3, 4, 6–8, 34, 78–79, 124–125, 167, 190
Native Americans. See Indian Wars
Nicaragua, 218
Normandy invasion. See D-Day

Office of Strategic Services (OSS), 132–134
Operation Ajax, 212
Operation Torch, 62

Pararescue Jumpers (PJs), 151, 159
Peacekeeping, 191–206
Pinkerton, Allan, 125
Plains of Abraham, 34, 55, 58, 123
Prisoners-of-war, 142, 143–147

Revolutionary War (American), vi, 11–12, 33–34, 56–58, 80, 99, 102, 123–124, 143, 187–189

Rifles, 99–102, 104, 106–107, 111, 112–113
RHIBs, 69
Robert, Henry M., 174
Roosevelt, Theodore, 36
Russia; Soviet Union, 3, 6–8, 10–11, 110–111, 129–130, 134–135, 213

Seabees, 179
SERE, 142
Siege tactics, 5–6
Snipers, 95–98
in history, 98–112
in today's military, 112–118
training of, 113–115
SOG, 215–217
Somalia, 193, 194
Soviet Union. See Russia; Soviet Union
Special Operations Command, 149–150, 207–209, 219–222
Special operations, history of, 210–218
Stalingrad, 8, 10
Stuart, J. E. B., 34, 81

Tanks, use of in war, 84–85, 88–93
Tarawa, 62
Task Force 5, 209
Task Force 20, 209
Task Force 121, 209, 222

10th Mountain
 Division, 39–41, 43,
 48, 49, 50, 51
Ticonderoga, 33, 169

Urban warfare
 fortifications and, 3,
 5–6
 history of, 3–14
 perils of, 1
 tactics of, 12–13,
 14–23
 training for, 2, 25–26
U.S. Air Force Special
 Operations, 209
U.S. Army, 14
U.S. Army Rangers, 43

U.S. Army Special
 Forces, 209
U.S. Cavalry, 82
U.S. Marine Corps, 14,
 43 51, 57, 65, 70, 72,
 111
USMC Force Recon, 62,
 67, 112, 209
U.S. Navy, 65, 67
U.S. Navy SEALS, 62,
 65, 67, 112, 209, 213,
 215

Verdun, 8, 9
Vietnam War, 28,
 42–43, 65, 85,
 111–112, 135, 147,

148–149, 167, 181,
 191, 215–218

Washington, George,
 11, 56–57, 123, 189
West Point, 33, 57–58,
 169–170
World War I, 8, 9, 12,
 36, 84–85, 107,
 126–128, 174–175
World War II, 8, 10–11,
 12–14, 39–42, 60,
 61–64, 85, 109–111,
 129–134, 175–179,
 210–211

Image Credits

Associated Press: 150; Dwight D. Eisenhower Museum: 176; French Ministry of Culture: 127; Imperial War Museum: 110, 130; Library of Congress: 4, 7, 9, 35, 83, 84, 86, 105, 124, 125, 133, 144, 172, 173; National Archives: 12, 13, 38, 42, 63, 109, 119, 134, 146, 148, 171, 181, 215; National Archives of Canada: 171; National Park Service: 103; North Wind Picture Archives: 3, 29, 58, 76, 79, 100; United States Department of Defense Photos: 2, 24, 44, 46, 69, 93, 192, 193, 194, 200, 202; United States Air Force: 87, 152, 160; United States Army: 20, 27, 40, 48, 50, 73, 90, 95, 183, 184, 186, 205, 211, 221; United States Army Corps of Engineers: 164, 178, 180, United States Marine Corps: 1, 2, 15, 16, 52, 66, 68, 113, 114, 116, 117, 141, 156, 157, 158, 162, 196, 197, 207; United States Navy: 71; White House Photos: 138.